I0158793

Surfing or Suffering ~ Together
*Sense * Consciousness*
Fields of a Body
With Streams and Stars of Hearts

Sunny Jetsun

**** You are a little Planet in Space ****

978-1-910363-43-0

Surfing or Suffering ~ Together
*Sense Consciousness * Fields of a Body*
With Streams and Stars of Hearts

Sunny Jetsun

Books by the Same Author:

Driving My Scooter through the Asteroid Field

Coming Down Over Venus ~ "Hallo Baba"

'Light love Angels from Heaven

New Generation, Inspiration, Revolution, Revelation

All the Colours of Cosmic Rainbows'

*'Green Eve * Don't lose the Light Vortex **

My brain's gone on holiday ~ free flowing feelings'

"When You're happy you got wings on your back ~

Reposez vos oreilles à Goa; We're only one kiss away"

'Psychic Psychedelic'

'Streaming Lemon Topaz Sunbeams'

*'Invasion of Beauty *FLASH* The Love Mudras'*

'Patchouli Showers ~ Tantric Temples'

It's Just a Story ~ We Are All The Sun ~ Sweet Surrender

Anthology #1 ~ 'Enjoy The Revolution'

Anthology # 2 ~ 'Love & Freedom ~ Welcome'

'He Lives In a Parallel Universe'

'Queen of Space ~ King of Flower Power ~ dripping Rainbows'

'All Love Frequency ~ In Zero Space'

Peace Goddess*Spirit of the Field*The Intimacy Sutras

'Heavenly Bodies ~ Celestial Alignments

Feeling ~ Energy that Is LOVE in Itself'

*'I've been to Venus & back*These Are Real Feelings**

*Let the Universe Guide Your Heart*through Space'*

The Kiss in Slaughterhouse 6

Books by the Same Author:

Originally Published as Ciel Rose

'Sadhu Sadhu Sadhu ~ "All Beings Be Happy" ~ Shanti Shanti'

'Trilogy of Vibrations ~ The Oneness of Life'

'Each Fragment of Life Is Sacred ~ These Are Your Children'

'Young Women Spin On Their Doorsteps At Dusk'

'Life Is Simple, Sharing ~ Loving Kindness from the Heart'

'The Universe Coming Across the River'

*

Originally Published as Sunny Revareva

*Pure Light ~Cosmic*Sweet Heart ~We've All Got Stars Inside.*

'Perfect Love ~ No Mind * Star Light ~ Come Alive'

'True Freedom ~ Natural Spiritual Beauty
*Here * Now ~ Gems of Eternity'*

*

This book is arranged from Surreal notes made from
Inspirational conversations with friends during
the 2006/07 winter season in Anjuna, Goa.
"Thank you all" ~ Om Shanti, Shanti

*

'In Lak'ech'

Is Mayan for 'I am another yourself'
A powerful concept embracing the notion that we are
all connected through the Energy and Flow of the Universe.
The galactic code of honour is to manifest and demonstrate harmony
by whatever means possible. Always playing by the rules of harmony at
the same time respecting local intelligence. The code's chief command,
to do nothing to further any notion of duality or separateness.

*

Jose Arguelles 'The Mayan Factor' 1996 (p.58) & Wikipedia.

Revolution at the barricades

"The purpose of Mindfulness and the four sublime states was
to neutralise the power of the ego that limits human potential.
Instead of saying "I Want" the Yogin would learn to seek the good
of others; Instead of succumbing to the hatred that is the result
of our self ~ centred greed; use compassion and good will.
When these positive, skillful states are Cultivated with Yogic
intensity, they can root themselves more easily in Unconscious
impulses of our Minds so becoming habitual. The Four Sublime states
are used to pull down the barricades we erect between ourselves
and others in order to protect the fragile ego."
('Buddha' ~ Karen Armstrong)

*

Bhakti Baba.

Living Life Free
Free free free free free free free free free free
Watering the seed, growing the flower
Cosmos of Stars in blossom
Filled with desire ~
Deep Inside you
blissful fire

*

*Kali*Maya can drive anyone Mad!*

I got a Text from England
*Daffodils * blooming ~*
Blackbirds are laying eggs
Longer days and Golden Sunsets
Find the Space
Allowing the FORM to be
You are the action ~
Free whirling, helping them go on the journey.
Everything is simple ~ natural
*as a Rock * Is God*

Raw Chocolate

10 times Stronger than the most passionate Kiss ~
You can do Amazing things with your Imagination.
Making conjugal, coital bliss, together high in Taipei.
tracked down by a passionate Angel on a love mission.
Umbilical tube Attached to North Goa (to Psy Baba)
One of those sorts of personalities & laughing Osho.
A Heart of Gold
Detached from the Turkish delight ~
Free of those Quantum strings, naked on the beach.
Need to find our true sense of self.
Does it have the Pull?

*

'Me Oh My'

Music ~ Spiritual House
Breaking it down more, nice melodies
Not just a beat, repeating a chant
Om Om Om Om Om Om Om
Seen through it ~ Don't want to get stuck in a game.
Meant to escape from fear & desire, at least be aware!
And enjoy what life brings as a Conscious human being.
You got to live your Life otherwise you're dependent.
Do You know what it is to be a True Queen?
A Love that Never dies

*

Taj * Mahal

§§§§§§§§§§§§§§§§§§§§
§§§§§§§§§§§One*Virus§§§§§§§§§§§
§§§§§§§§§§§§§§§§§§§§§§§§
§§§§§§§§§§§ Away from extinction §§§§§§§§§§§
It's all goin' on in Goa ~Tao, being here now ~
light gravity, light density, right now it can an also be
shattered dreams on the broken backs of crimson butterflies

< Buddha Is A Concept >

Developed in the Mind; Where else? From Outer space!
Is energy a concept, is Life, is feeling, is Love for you,
Is Vibration, is birth, is death, is God, is the Universe?
Is it Cosmic boundlessness, consciousness of nothingness?
Everything Manifest is a 'concept' of what? Receiving Maya!
Where does it Originate? Into fields of sense consciousness,
*with streams & stars of hearts * through dying processes ~*
Is that a concept too?

*

Cliffs

"In the land
of the blind,
the one eyed
man is king"

*

wikileaks.com

If you are the biggest Weapons manufacturer on the Planet.
You will need to Sell those new Weapons of 'Mass or Meno'
destruction to someone! You will Need a Reason to USE them.
"Know the unknowable ~ merge into Impermanent Brahma"

*

Subliminal Probe

Can she take you seriously after crashing your
new rickshaw that you got in your dowry?
Enjoying Hampi just after the Monsoon!
Touching hot Russian Sputniks last night.
That subconscious Old Chestnut!
Getting wound up with nothing ~
Party drug, do or die; In chill out huts.
"I use them, don't let them use me"
From the Twilight zone of her Terminal Pain.
The will to continue to Live for her young children,
when you have to let go on a Morphine Cocktail!

Chick on a stick
'Made to Order'
"blah, blah, blah
doing things with sheep,
ba ba ba"
A precious drop of self-survival
*

A Clone Shock
To leave Goa very insular ~
Would you take your wife seriously
if she wore human skulls around her neck?
She's not a biter taking his face off!
Aiming for the Heart.
A crack in the dream
Mirror of my feelings ~
It's a shock to the brain!
Tunnel vision of Love in a chain gang.
*

US
'Adopt Another Highway'
*

Radio Atlantis
'Amrit laya' > the Stateless State
Nectar of Immortality ~
Feeding the Universe
"Beauty in the Mind of a Beholder"
OK are you overworked and underpaid?
Surrounded by ecstatic, Quantum Angels
*

Witch Doctor Style!
'Can take you out of your mind'
And it's a natural high! Drumming…
It says something about the messenger ~
"Got stuck in Anjuna travellin' around India!"

What makes the Giant Sequoia trees grow so big?
Isis Bhakti Osiris Bhakti Aphrodite Bhakti
Eros Bhakti Orpheus Bhakti Venus Bhakti
Shakti Bhakti Shiva Bhakti Jesus Bhakti
'Still waters run deep'

*

Who said, "One shouldn't cry over spilt blood?"
Underneath the laughter you can find your tears.
Understanding of the eternal Mind; Is it possible?
We like dropping them but don't like them dropped on us!
7/7, 9/11's is everyday in the Middle East; have the people
lost their rights like in the US? Terrorists left, right & centre!
Bombs dropping around your head makes you really dead.
Blown to bits again; Not in Baghdad but Birkenhead ~
"You could go out in the Blackout without being mugged;
the Luftwaffe blew up my mother's house and Sweet shop!"

*

*Tag * A Perfect World*
Entrance & Exits, a revolving door "This is what comes through to us"
Have to listen to the Silence ~ "be open and it will come naturally"
"better to have loved and lost than to never have loved at all"
That's not true because you never lose in deeper vibrations.
Melt down fear, body die ~ Atman fly
Over the edge of the Milky Way

*

*Full Space: Words invoking mantras, incantations * incarnations.*
Bombarded by spells in your cells. mixing genes & chemicals.
From being at the Top to being dumped at the bottom, hard!
It's a great feeling; get ripped apart, have to repair your-self.
Everyone gets this test Universal, the test is realising that
'Your greatest attachment can be your deepest Pain!'
*Lotus flowers in a pond * bitten by a snake on the arse ~*

A Hyper-Myth

Just to say, 'this is how I feel'
& I need to express it to you ~
Reconnection, It's already there.
Free spirit in the moment ~ Released.
Be happy ~ with what you choose to do.
Fear of rejection is an unrealistic response.

*

Paradise Rushing

I thought if I closed my eyes, I wouldn't wake up!
Being catatonic in a psychedelic room wondering
If this place would ever change again in my Mind.
A delusion of a black hole, have to let it go ~ flow
It's not a Brain seizure, heart attack or mini stroke.
*Separated my*self from myself, scary detachment.*
Lost in space but you knew it's a trip ~

*

Rio's Gay Parade

"A couple of our lads, have been mugged there!"
Cocktails on Copacabana, 'Universo Parallelos'
The best lookin' lesbians, transgenders in the World!
"She gave me freedom to do what I wanna do"
Single life ~ can be great, for meeting angels

*

Fucking for Money

If it's someone you like, a Massive bonus!
I Love travellin' on my own. 'Gift her a Monster cock!'
The girls there all on 'Ice', crystal Meth. chaotic Moods!
Worse than Heroin!
Can you bake a chocolate chip cookie?
"I Like Reality"
"Never doing a line of powder without a beer"
He knows what it's like, getting stuck in a Coke corner....

<u>Angels' New Vegalistas Light</u>
Tree's Axis of the World
Caduceus' symbol of Divine Life & ~
Patriarchs from the Genesis taken command!
Golden Serpents incarnating forces of nature,
life principles conquered by a Rationale cut ~ off.
Shamans diving deep into molecular sweep of currents
Reactions ~ being of Inspiration & Wonder
"The Point Is there is No Point It's always changing"
"Music is the path to the spirits" ask Anatta for directions.
Zeus came with his daughter, Princess Dream Sequence.
DNA. on her tongue rolling round your spacious Neocortex.
'Gaining access to knowledge of the Vital Principle'

*

<u>Embracing the Universe as an 'Ideology' of Cosmic humanity/humility</u>
'Estimated observable atoms in the Universe 10 to the power 30.'
In All living species Proteins are made up of exactly the same 20 Amino
acids (small molecules)."If we stretched out the DNA. in the nucleus
of a human cell we'd get a two yard long thread that is 10 atoms wide;
it is one billion times longer than its own width. DNA. is approximately
120 times narrower than the smallest wavelength of visible light"
('Cosmic Serpent' ~ Jeremy Narby)

*

"How you use it or abuse it….." You're taking the piss dear!
*Chemical marriage Alchemy ~ resonating * Hydrogen exploding.*
Dualism of the Sun & Moon inside one Universe.
Source streaming only reflections of the sunlight
turning white blue into golden auras.
Then I stood up and asked, "where is your heart man?"
The Military says, 'it's only an optical illusion, step back, go to sleep'
that 1km spaceship landed in the kitchen! I don't believe them,
it's hovering, Orange glowing lights outside on the tiled roof.
Orgasmatic-Mind mirroring back the radiance of basic truth.
Russian UFO. Technologies & Buddha field harmonies ~

Dukkha Disharmony

"He's not feeling as he used to feel"
"I might as well talk to the wall"
This doesn't belong to me, let go tight grip on Pride & Ego.
Come to stage of detachment, witness the Mind from Itself!
Change of growth & decay, blooms in your lovely bouquet.
Watching the disintegration of a mountain, cycling of birth,
death; seed becomes a sapling becomes a tree unending.
No permanency of the seeming unity of being ~
"Tendency to change is inherent in all things"
It's got a life of its own ~ electrons spinning in orbits
*Multi*dimensional Expansion at the speed of light..*
Golden Pagodas illuminating 100,000,000 Galaxies
Sustaining every plant and animal, thank You Sun.
Earth Our Jewel in the Sky

*

A flirting Mare

Roxanne riding on the back of Tantrically tempted Aristotle.
"If she can do that to me Imagine what she can do to you
my King?" He decided to come to India for the Spirituality.
Came with a lot of slave girls from all around the Planet
to impress a naked Yogi, who'd renounced even himself!
Fragrant Persian lust walking alone in her Palace garden.
Where is the path of true happiness your royal highness?

*

Culture Slash

'Live and Let Live in Empathy'
Brilliant Indian respect ~ aspect.
"Where is the Spiritual Programming?"

*

Rays from the Stars

Waiting for Shiva ~
Heart beats in the Sky

<u>Glib disclaiming democratic doctrine</u>
Only wanted to be at the top table, with Bealzibub.
Blame, complain, shame of a wrong sexy Dossier;
fed from the BBC, all the News Stations stating Untruths.
Medea's Labour Government run by corrupt, 'illegal' Idiots.
Speaking for view of a New World Order's Global Empire.
A Cabinet of greedy buffoons with no Real awareness ~
Mindsets, now looking for excuses, an escape from
'The Total Corruption of Power' – 'Disaster Looming'.
Dysfunctional footprints ~ giving No answers
'Making It all up as they went along!'

*

Definition of Spiritual ~ Why not have what you like…
And let the Universe support those little swimming tadpoles?
Can get into trouble, don't need any bleach on the beach!
Planet's gonna blow up, Nature's gonna fuck up;
floating downhill with a dizzy blonde, thank God!

*

Be Alert! they never knew it anyway, people forget, they never
saw it coming from around the next corner; expecting anything!
Nice to wake up with blue skies & trees, shimmering greens.
Everyone knows of Psychedelic Krishna & the telly tubbies.
"Step off the carousel and become a Buddha"
Angelic Devas enjoying the light
"I feel brighter every day"
Why believe the stuff that marches us to War?
"Live and Let Live" ~ simply so other's simply live.
Is that your Password?
The longer you live here, the more you get it, Goa.
Spinning at speeds of light inside your 'Mer ka ba'.
Vortex shortcuts to Heaven on a golden ball.
Fast Track etheric body channeling ~
'Consciousness not Information'
Everything Is Allowed

Tiarés of Infinite Joy

She was wearing a pareo of gardenias ~
Labouring with Love all the way from Tonga.
Brought contraband across dark gigantic waves.
Excitement building around the fire.
"What happens the Morning after?"
Going for the 80% Incapacity Benefit…
Pretending to be a shaking forklift truck driver!
21/11/2007 £50 Million Aid to Palestine, millions more to Africa
And our Pensioners get a £1 a week rise from the Government!
15/2/2003: One Million people marched Against the Iraq War.
Lies, spinning the 'Truth of Real Politick'; Absolutely No WMD!
Blair's new fascism, blood All over his hands; believed in War!
"The people we were fighting decided to fight back!"
Extraordinarily rendered we were led down the GB. Swanee, Oh Yeah!
Owning up to A Massive Betrayal - In the Grip of FOX TV. BBC News!
Ignorantly he channeled the Devil's dark Magic, here's your host Dr. Faust.

*

Solar needs & seeds

Temple of Full Love ~ Atlantis
Ascended Masters living in Innocence ~
Lady Nadar appeared with an enneagram on her brow.
Drawn upon the Uncensored Creative
Impulses of the Unconscious

*

Time's Up Ali Baba

Backing a 'No Plan' is Criminal Negligence of Intelligence!
A history of 'Criminals against Humanity', off White House.
Robbing all the Antiquities of our Babylonia ~
"Were there that many vases being looted?"
They let a country of 25 million Collapse!
The Phone Exchange was bombed by a B52
No Protection, No Communication, Anarchy!
On the streets of Baghdad, they let the rats run wild

Please don't Break an Occupied Country

Imposed by deadly force sanctions for 10 years by the UN.
Destroying All the Goodwill in their hearts & Minds ~
And starved one million children; A Complete Failure!
'To be seen that everyone is treated equally under the Law'
Four million people, 90,000 children, 6% of population on a
DNA register, the first and biggest in the World, Mein Fuhrer!
What about the young woman from Qataf; Saudi Arabian who
was gang raped! The Judge asked if she was wearing her Veil
and ordered her to be lashed 200 times for making an appeal!
Is It possible to achieve absolute mental, physical clarity ~
neither perception nor non-perception in a Yogic trance?
Found No release in asceticism; took them to the Ultimate
Level and still failed ~ Enjoying, be happy in truest sense.
A moment of Spontaneous Compassion had helped lead
him outside his own selfish ego into sweet fulfilled Rapture.
Suffering brings a Spiritual maturity, if you want to accept it,
not suppress, repress, oppress, obsess, deny, reject it. Facing it
the preoccupation with the Self ~ the prison of our own Ego.
Letting the Identification, conditioning, austerities, dissolve ~
Way to enter the depth of the Psyche ~
1st Jnana ~ ecstasy in the Uruvela forest...
Selfless empathy brought him a moment of Spiritual Release,
experiencing the coolness of Nibbana under a Rose Apple tree

*

'Addiction'

"Shouldn't fight it ~
make Peace with it"

*

Osho's Bluebirds

"Love is a bridge ~ cross it don't build your house on it."
'Love turns to hate in an instant.' Shiva's Gratefully Dead track.
Goa where to go to get the free Madness amongst friends...
"I've Lost My Mind!"

Pure Delight

Nothing much to do with greedy craving but having the Awareness
of it ~ Is there a need to Fight your Human Nature as an ascetic?
Distrusting Joy, Why? Habitual behaviour ~ Your Upbringing…
Working with Human Instinct, not fighting against it ~
Amplifying States of Mind Conducive to enlightenment.
Needing a Sense of seclusion for Trance, be of it not in it,
fostering such +ve states of wholesome Mind (Kusala).
Disinterested Compassion, cultivating energetic +ve attitudes
Promoting Spiritual Health, gentle harmony, Loving Kindness.
Right talk, countering feelings of ill will and Violence.
Take Delight in Possessing the bare minimum ~
2nd nature

*

Could be Self-Destructive

No emotional self indulgence or extreme ascetism ~
Mindfulness scrutinising his behaviour, emotions, feelings,
consciousness, witness the rise & fall of Material body & mind.
'Anicca' ~ Not neurotic, Compulsive, Obsessive Introspection.

*

Get to Know Your Nature

'Dukkha's' Views of suffering & distortion seed.
Leading you to enmity, guilt & ravenous greed ~
"When our desires clash with the cravings of others,
gives more Selfish desire, hatred and misery darling!
Clinging to things not giving any lasting satisfaction.
She's constantly discontented with the Present ~
Insights of new clarity from Samadhi Concentration.

*

'Desdedanya'

See you later alligator
See you later Indian Tiger
See you later Elephant ~
See you later Yangtze Dolphin

Malevolence - See things as they really are!
Banishing hatred from his body, mind and heart ~
No ill will & full of compassion through Meditation.
'Metta' ~ Love feeling of no hatred. Purify your Mind ~
Non-attached & Transcend in acts of Total Compassion.
Fill sense conditioned energy fields with love & kindness
Not possessing us in Needs, desires, wild ecstatic coitus.
Meditation, helping us to be clear ~ seeing the distractions
depriving us of Peace. Darling do you realise our ephemeral
intercourse, the nature of these Invasive thoughts and cravings
in your breast; tending to Identify with them less & less emotion.
Seeing them as 'Mine' so they're less disturbing to you & me.
Being blind doesn't mean you have to be Unaware ~ 'Anatta'

*

Travelling in Your Mind's Eye
Expand the Mind, setting the Mind Free
Infinite Consciousness of eternal Space.
Release the Mind From the selfish Cravings ~
Poisoning us in my needs and Desires for you!
Seeing my life as part of the human race schema.
As part of the Planet Earth, as part of the Cosmic ~
Enjoying it for what it is ~ Glorious & delirious Maya!
With real laughter, real Innocence, real truth & Love

*

Everything in the Universe is Alive
Each day dreaming into being, making it Sacred
** in Zero Point fields ~ of a Nature Power place **
Magic sleeping in the Earth waiting for its release.
Stepping on the bridge between the scene & unseen.
Caressing your juicy matter & your panting spirit darling.
Inside the Palace of the Pimp, you can buy the best Opium
from the Royal guard! Or from the Kashmiris selling up the road.
Observing through a key hole ~ he could see the Karma Sutra
Unfolding, he's a Yogic sage, beyond all senses, Sat chit ananda

Cups of Magic Revolution

Reached Senanigama by the Neranjara river ~
Happily playing under a Bodhi tree with Sujata.
Reality transcending his rational understanding.
The last drop ~ apprehended directly, profoundly.
Identified 'Dhamma' Integrated into one's own life.
Egotism makes us horrible to others, distorting vision.
Still living with the relative pain in perfect equanimity ~
Getting rid of the cravings & Ignorant States of Mind.
Direct Knowledge of a ficus leaf & the Coitus Lotus.

*

General Colin Powell - Top Dog at Calamity Central

"What we're giving you are facts and conclusions
based on solid Intelligence"- Duck, flying Spuds!!!
'Shocked & Awed alright!' & we've Launched Your
Worst nightmares in Less than 45 seconds!
"They're running the World!" If you let them.
That's what I call a very diabolical, dark Spark!
& She was to be flogged for calling a teddy bear Mohammed.
Put behind bars for fuckin' blasphemy! What does that tell You?

*

Bodh Gaya, late spring 528 BC

Becomes perfectly human ~ not reacting, liberating himself.
Modulated into his 1st Jnana under a shaded Banyan tree.
His 'Yathabhuta' ~ his Awakening, free from Samsara.
Took a rest at the 3 stations, 'Sila, Samadhi, Panna…
Things as they Really are ~ Dhamma par excellence.
'Atra' ~ With the Insight of Peace and fulfillment
Elucidated fundamentals governing ~ Life of the Cosmos.
Seeing it and Knowing it through experiences & searching
for the Truth, be HAPPY in Yourself, Super Energetically.
Does it really work? "This is what I've got to work with ~
A Spirit of total Self-abandonment; it makes perfect sense
GO"

Or Falling Apart!
So don't lose touch with this inner centre.
*Oriented * Artists becoming fully Creative*
When did you see the Oceans Rust?
Facing to the East on an Axis of the Cosmos ~
In Peace, perfect balance, without Limitations
Final fight of Maya ~ a delusion not to die!

*

*Axis Mundi Point where all * contradictions are balanced*
Do I have these Qualities to Live by; Am I Real, is it true?
Touching the ground, Mother nature, with his right hand,
deepest Affinity between Earth & Selfless human beings
in tune, channeling the basic laws of Universal existence.
Two passing meteorites falling in subconscious bliss ~
Live from the Heart ~ blazing in their Cosmic kiss

*

Brahma's Ahimsa Projections
Feeling the pain & suffering of others ~ empathically,
deepening yourself, so realising this noble truth.
Truest essence of dhamma ~ feeling compassion for others.
Open to the Direct Knowledge until being one with it darling.
Nibbana's Gates Open to Everyone ~ wholly Integration
One with it ~ Into Infinity
A compassion & kindliness offensive, diffusing hostilities.
Qualities of an Arhant, feeding the river ~ fresh flowers

*

A Logic Bomb On Oxford Street
'Stenography' ~ hiding something in plane sight.
"Taking down the Global senses of satellite systems;
I'm not asking for Permission!"
She's dead, whatever you say now doesn't matter ~
In the face of Adversity having the latest Intelligence.
"Waiting on a Dirty, Radio Active Bomb for Xmas!"
Found out she was a double Agent!

'Obsession'

To besiege, to haunt, preoccupy the Mind of ~
To trouble (as an evil spirit)

*

Adding to your Wish List

Partnered to support a Common cause
Organic bouquets sold where 5% goes to 'Adopt A Minefield!'
Isn't that Surreal, as Dorothea Tanning's visual poetry?
You can find Diego Rivera's 'Flower Sellers' at a Target,
near you! Those Hallucinatory, Projected elements.
Calla lilies sold in the markets of Teotihuacan.
'In Lake'ch' ~ "I Am another yourself"
The Mayan Code of Honour

*

Global Demeter

My mother goes to Ireland for her homemade bread
Light emerging needs & seeds of Lotus eaters.
Sparkles of a mirrored bauble, 3 dimensional
jade head of the Sun God found in a maize field.
Hunahpu & Xbalanque bringing them back to life ~
Their father came out of a cracked open Tortoise shell.
Could have been worse, could have been born in Belsen!
And Mother was born in a sweetshop by the Dolly mixtures.
Sirian Archaeologists found a Blue Tooth buried in the sand.
"You're all right lounging about on a beach all day, yapping"
"I knew you were going to come up with that one sooner or later"
Representing a Divine entity, Pachamama called being here now.
*Welcome to the land of Chac * Mool eating Charley's heart.*
Dishing up an offering from the Red Jaguar throne.

*

Think what you like! 'Free Ticket' > Conditions Apply!
Capitalism > 'It does the trick' for Soros not for davidicke.com
Mega profiteers Rothschild's, Rockefellers, Bildebergers etc.
Dodgy Carlyle Capital Corp; defaulted $16.6 billion. 6/3/2008.

Being involved not attached

All the World's media complicit in the fake, official 9/11 narrative
Bringing in the Patriot Act, Homeland Security another Terrorist War!
Trying to instill Martial LAW without naming it that, no rights in a Police state!
Governing by a clique of Masons; Admirals and Chief Constables' night out!
Secret Societies, Insider Trading, lift the stumps and take it for a ride.
You can get to a point where you don't think about that other person.
This is a song I wrote at my ranch with an old aborigine living on it.

*

EROTIC WEAPONS

Hi-Tech Neutron bombs, very subtle ways of killing us all!
Krishna now he's got all the amore not Jihadi Johnny!
He opens his mouth and says ~ "I am the Universe"
There's five million people walking around America
dressed as a super-hero, one on every corner!

*

They have their minions who don't know what's going on.
You have your rights but here you're in their Legal System.
I can help you but I can't help you commit a crime me Lud.
Caution me and tell me what crime I have committed.
If you're caught there is a procedure, none of it is true.
It's a game of Legalese, you're there by deception.
You're read your rights, you have the right to remain silent but
everything that you say will be taken down and may be used
AGAINST YOU

*

The Dog's Bollocks - We the people for the people

They wrote the American constitution on Hemp!
It's done by consent, protecting us from a nasty Empire.
"I've carried this seed around in my spirit since I was born.
It's all bullshit, the Mars' landing was filmed in Alaska, USA.
A $multi trillion fraud, NASA, Pentagon, Weaponised business!
Continued Investments in the biggest Global 'Death' Industries!

I'll have you removed

You're a Public servant, taken an Oath to Protect my Rights.
You sir have duties and responsibilities whilst in that uniform.
They're all in the Law Society everything is about procedure.
Challenged the Judge so he couldn't go through the procedure.
You can have your opinion but I'm talking about the Law of the Land.
He'll leave as he has no jurisdiction if you never committed a crime.
They'll never show you the game, blatant deception, hidden reality.
"If I suffer a loss someone's committed a crime, robbing y/our energy"
They can kill us all with a push of a button, by flicking a delete switch.
Natural Law, the Law of the Land Not Maritime Law, Law of the Sea ~
It's Commercial Law and doesn't apply to us, as you well know me Lud!
Oppressing us with our Ignorance, paying the system, voluntary rip-off!
If you don't say anything that's accepted as consent, joinder.
This is my jurisdiction not yours now fuck off!

*

Mindset: A /14C -1

They tested my dad for asbestosis & Mesothelioma.
People, forget all about the Rations, the Conditionings.
The War's over my Sovereign! Raytheon-can you hear?
"Fear is a sickness, infection don't let it under your skin"
Tune into Cosmogony, to Polar Bears, dolphins, Tigers,
Honey Bees and All the other endangered species ~
Transmuting Amazonia into a barren Atacama desert.
OK if you like only camels and scorpions with no Oasis...
Living in times of perpetual foggy mirage and burning clouds.
Red hot children ~ with Crocidolite in a crimson Death Valley.

*

Myth: Perfect God Teflon fights Irresistible Queen Karma

Even Superman had his Kryptonite factor No. 7
Achilles his heel, Narcissus his super Id ego,
Henry had his eight wives' heads to sort out!
Salvador Allende his Kissinger & Pinochet shadowy ghosts.
Tony Blair's Hell, his zeal to invade & conquer, 'Righteously!'

*More Astronomical*Cosmic Info*

Krishna's Celebration not your Mind's suffering
take the Unconditional path if you want to go ~
"The only time when a man was enlightened
On a battlefield!"
In only 18 verses, Krishna sang it.
She was part of you, nothing else ~
"Krishna lives in Virginia in the Taj Mahal of the west"
He's not meditating on anything, he is the whole.
Sounds of the Magic Flute in the forest.
Just got a smiley from my Bhakti App. ~ sent me an SMS.
Why Choices, was it like this or like that; who cares?
Visual poetry not Steganography

*

Nothing to do with Womb Magic

A moustache promises authority in Mid East & Mid west!
Meditation ~ Emoto's magic quality of Intentional Images.
~ distorted treatment of perspective, of reality.
Surrealists jetting chance elements into their work ~
feeling Inspiration from the first line of a love poem.
& disconnections ~ cut a bunch of bananas inside a glass office.
*'Nude woman in a Red armchair' reading the 'Auto*biography*
of an Embryo' ~ Liberating sexual convention.
Sensuous physicality, 'Freedom from Tradition'
Unplugging > the Mind

*

*Beyond Supra*Realism*

'1936, London International Surreal Exhibition'.
Francis Bacon's 'Figures in a garden' Rejected ~
"as insufficiently surreal" ~ Reality even only a line -
*Out of context * Giving shocks to the habitual system.*
Zen enlightened moment on a Miro canvas, being Alive.
Twombly's lovely colour fragrances of abstract seasons

Liberated from the Competitive Conditioning Programme

Time marked by dehumanising conflicts - switching gears.
Reflection of something, is that a new idea? Control by fears.
Freud had a view of Primal drives or was that a girl in tears?
I liked Jung's Archetypes, more like Osho's Celebration.
New sense of the human propensity for Brutality; Jesus!
Cultural psychology or aestheticism of Art for Mr. Klimt?
Such a beautiful painting of an abstract Orange orchard.
Did it have something to do with the New ballet of Atoms
existing in your Imagination or knowing your real brain
has a life of its own & likes to travel into forest corners?
Did you understand any truth from 'The Golden Flower',
feel a new moon rising in 'Le Poète Allongé' de Chagall?
But Art is not the same as Cosmic Spirit is it?
Man or Star? Ask a Mayan

*

Giotto came to Padua and Orvieto

Raphael's poetry, Signorelli's Apocalypse ~
Italian customs making Dualism into Art & Opera
And a Roman Temple looking sublimely beautiful
from every vantage point of a Villa Rotonda.
Verdi & Puccini creating ~ Unknown eternal essence
"I'm not just a drop ~ I am the Ocean"
beyond the limitation, within & beyond
bubbles bubbling ~ You are
no need to do anything.
No Plans, Dead Peace, Revelation.
New identification ~ not identifying
with the senses, even the Mind-Yours.
Realisation of No Separation
'Immaculate Completeness'

*

CCTV > 'In Court for Obstructing a Train'
"Had a drink like! Yu knoooww...."

All Equal

No big
*no little * parts*
On the Ocean
even the Mind is a sense.
Where are You ~
'Master' of our own Mind
what we have to learn?
Don't constrict Yourself
Can't find a Point
Where You start, begin or end
Perfect ~ You are no body, ego less
*no competition * being the Rock too.*
You are the In-dweller transforming.
Can't define ~ putting a boundary
around is a Limit, a restriction.
Willing not to know ~ Judging it
Separating their feelings from other's
Patterns

*

Mindless (being happy)

A no Knowing
just a being
Without any Me ~
no need to be better
no competition, struggle.
Milarepa jumping off a cliff - what dies?
Energy leaves your body
You lose nothing ~
Broke his body of Light
Smashed all his Illusions.
Too caught up in Egosyntonic Identity
disorder (No need to commit Suicide).
"You're a process of living ~ dying"

A Fuck, a Cook, Cleaner and a Nurse

Three people standing there ~ vibrating
Nature's sounds in the depths of the forest.
You can't hide anything on the dance floor ~
Best not to know because we don't know anything
We only think we do! Dark energy Space is what?
Identifying with all their suffering, driving the Ego.
A perspective pointing at a pure perception.
Rock my world Baby; We are the Best!
When it's the right time for us it's the right time.
Fuck everything! They got the Black Box…
Its full Love ~ eternally changing

*

Modern Warfare

There is Abundance ~ it's all been hidden.
They're into taking as much as they can out of it for themselves.
Try not to believe anything you're told.
Manufactured consent coming from the Insiders.
& they get their food and wood from the jungle ~
Sleeping on a bamboo mat,
Live & Learn.

*

Cosmic Debt

Being robbed blind, making the most 'Lawful Rebellion'
You're classified 'Dead' now owned by the Government.
'I am a LIVING PERSON I have my Divine Given Rights'
Once you get your head through that veil of Holy Bullshit!
It's a construct, web, matrix, we've all been stitched up!
We're all heads of our own State, God made all of us.
Taking back our Authority, sharing, communicating it.
She's shaking her Spear at the Dragon of Ignorance!

*

First glimpse
Mind, Mind, Mind.
Do not refer to
what you think.
Witnessing rather
than A Separating ~
the Identity has to be Smashed
that's the Pain ~ ego's game
breaking the Illusion, delusion
Pierces through the Rock.
Om is not really a sound ~
Mantra getting into a pattern
where there is no mind ~
As long as it's nonsense,
terrified to let go
and play in Space.
I'm exhausted
Want to Know
What's Real

*

Memory
Reality is based
on the past
future ~ wave is a notion
present ~ wave is motion
we're all waves
of the Ocean

*

The Pain teaches
no stepping out
be in it
In the middle ~ of the pain
*there is no pain * beyond the senses*

<u>Ocean Waves</u>

No past, no imaginary future
no Universe ~ apparent Illusion
*Emptiness * Space is the Real…*
As soon as you make yourself breakable
You are weak! Developing Information
to destroy 'Knowledge'.
You Are Reincarnated
Right now ~
In everything
truth within

*

<u>Plighted to ~ A Diamond</u>

Sleeping with Venus in a high Power point
holding the deep Red crystal in your heart
Conscious of the Limits
of the Sense body
A Shell ~ then it goes
changes to the True essence
the true being ~ of no fear dear

*

<u>Exacto</u>

Bella Lucrezia Borga in the Aphrodisiac Palacio at Mantua.
We express what we feel
the last Fantastic supper.
"The Observer of the Mind is Me, I am not the Mind"

*

<u>Whose Gorgeous Bomblet!</u>

The Dow Company of Michigan, USA ~ made 'NAPALM!'
Their most (In)famous Death Product; what can you say?
So much of it dropped on people by Your Government!!
Why couldn't they keep giving us 'Saran Wrap' instead?
1967, 500,000 US. troops in Viet Nam, feeling it in the air!
Soldiers coming home from the battlefield….

Going with the change

Where is the end of something?
Knowing when it's time to leave you darling!
Using mirrors at the right place of no separation.
What makes something unique? nothing at all!
Enjoying Tao ~ Ego of joy, knowing same, same difference.
Training an Ego for a Virtual reality Identity, take your pick!
But it's inhuman to drop cruising nuclear bombs or napalm
demonic clusters with no daisies, on your wedding cake!
Are you discriminating? What values are you creating
*in your mind now? ~ 'Truth is all one' ~ It Is * As I Am*

*

Naturally Sunreal <:> in Front of the Sky

A nano-second, sleep-walking above the steelwork's high cranes at night.
What's the difference between a human & a feeling Android from Venus?
It's a Rocket fired from out of an underground bunker called CyberSaiBaba
A man's life falls apart and he throws himself off a suspension bridge!
Putting the pieces together, prescribed ~ a Wonderful Life is Heartfelt,
not for a Vengeful Gladiator enraged at a feast of Jealous Tyrants!
The scope of bloodlust is Unbelievable even to a normal Maniac.
Why did you try to stop a war Krishna if it's all the same?
Looking into something from the Cosmos ~ (big window)

*

Life Time Reflecting Light

Moving energies into magnetic prairies
Stardust falling through every pore & more
*effects of dark matter * full of faerie magick.*
What's the most open in Creation ~ Sahasha
Comes from the guts, comes along the main Ghats.
Open Mind ~ Closed Mind Changing Mind Still ness.
How much music of the spheres is in subatomic skies?
Opening to Rose petals, Open to miracles of birth & death
Open to transcendental ~ heart feelings in Cosmic strings.
Infinite expansion infinite expansion infinitely

Embracing All of You
Celebrate life in all its forms
Ego just let it be ~ naturally
Shit Happens If you want it to
*being happy Psy-trance * Shiva's dance*
even for a nano-second be in Space
Step off your bed of rusty nails
making something out of nothing with your life.
Photons of light streaming in ~
from behind the neutron curtain
Patterns of a day of sunshine
blossoming in your open heart

*

*Co * Existing*
Celebrating life in all its Forms
I married an infatuated egoist
I divorced a selfish narcissist
forever & ever & ever
Treasure

*

Putin's Moscow Rules
"Vote for who You Trust"
"Depends to which Standard you are being held up to"
A very low turnout for a Landslide!

*

Brazilian Bombshell, wet & free
"Promise of an exotically glamorous land ~
populated by beautiful women full of Samba
and bananas, growing as big as their nipples!
Ethnically loaded by virtue of her gleaming skin.
A descendent of Slaves, she emerged out of the big dipper.
Her Mother's name was written in a Mayan Star Sign
An easy going Paradise, not political but totally human"
"Did you ever listen to just the sound of waves?"

That Qatif Girl's Lips Are Sealed

Revealed, caught in the wake of a human rights disaster.
Sharia laws keeping Riyadh executioners' swords sharp
in this age of Blue tooth, seems medieval & very uncouth.
Male Predators getting away with Gangbanging a girl
in daylight and taking digital film on their mobile phones!
It certainly wasn't meant to be like that was it, Prophet?
This Ordeal condoned by Saudi Arabian Misogynic life.
She was Raped and suffers more intolerable, cruel strife.
Ordered to have 90 lashes, rose to 200 on appeal; Unreal!
To be flogged by a prison official with a Koran under his arm.
The Judge of Appeal Court said he'd have given her Death!
Her brother tried to kill her for the family's name shame.
A Woman's crime under 'Khalwa' law, of being outside
alone without a male relative ~ dictator to oversee her.
"You see she broke the 'law on Mingling' begetting evil"
Demonised by a fanatic, intolerable Police 'Commission
for the Propagation of Virtue and the Prevention of Vice'
Authority's using rape and torture to control a population.
It looks like the woman banged up in Sudan for calling
a teddy bear Mohammed, got off too lightly; screaming...
Many wanted her executed for blasphemy, in God's name!

*

Perfect Law of Liberty

Meditation ~ on the Courage,
to take the risk ~ of devotion

*

*Kaam & Rati * life happens*

Life It continues through the sexual act
Its Purest energy ~ Creating Life ~
That's how the Universe gets its Life!
The Goddess goes out into the Cosmos ~
Shiva residing in the Crown Chakra of everyone.
Raindrops in the Ocean

No Wing Diktat

*"There was no time anymore ~ just me floating along"
Why not give them away, sultry, naked Cro-Magnon women
walking through a noetic land of enchantment and dinosaurs.
You have a highly developed sense of beauty, erotic & exotic,
& are extremely intelligent, visiting the Acropolis, Theseion,
Temple of Jupiter, the tomb of Socrates, Heliopolis, Giza.
"It was poetic and of no time or place known to man,
the boat itself was the only link to reality"
"At that moment I was Free of possessions, Free of all ties ~
Free of fear, envy and malice" - "Out of this fiery anarchy
came the lucid healing, metaphysical speculations which today
enthrall the world." Henry Miller, at the Colossus of Maroussi.
"I could have passed quietly from one dream to another,
owning nothing, regretting nothing, wishing nothing."
"Magic is never destroyed the most we can do is cut
ourselves off, amputate the mysterious antennae
which serve to connect us with forces beyond our
Power of Understanding"
"Being communicated over and above language,
over and above personality;
something Magical which we recognise in dream"
"I had everything a man could desire and I knew it"
My blood was roaring with desire, full of pollination.
Went to the roots of a wild Olive bowed before a fruitless War*

*

*'Streptococcus Pneumoniae' living inside a bacteria haze.
Smoking chillums ~ "keeping your mantra" transcendence.
So why bother, why do it? ~ 'Got married on the battlefield!'
Kaleidoscopic wizardry, breaking the magic spell of language
Succeeding in destroying the power of illusion, took a nice trip.
Near death experiences; Sphinxes telling us to Snap out of it!
Deeper harmonies, deeper fulfillment, deeper joy in you.
How to be Fully alive <:> Spirituality is in perfect harmony*

What Do You want to Manifest?

Things come and go, Space remains forever & forever ~
The Bible, the Pyramid with a diamond on top of its Apex.
The Parthenon, the Coliseum, a heap of bleaching bones.
A Gothic Church, a Cathar Massacre enacted on its steps.
A Blind Pope's Telescope, for the Sun and Constellations.
A Mona Lisa, without her enigmatic ~ smiling at you.
A remodernised Guernica, a Rock & Roll Band
Yoga headstand, looking in a five-way mirror….
Debbie turning up on Venus with a Taoist genius.
As a nothingness

*

Mythical

They discovered how to light a fuse under 'Ideal light' Vishnu.
They learnt how to Direct market share of Shiva, Shakti, for the
factory & decided 'Rationally' to fully Exploit ~ Globally Brahma.
People needed a large chunk of money to sacrifice to their Egos.
Gave everyone a 'Free' bonus of Everlasting need for greed.
Hanging their hearts like dead animals in the Sun.

*

Inter-Active Seaside

Perfect fit, fits Perfectly, Perfectly fitting.
What are you doing with your time; Spending it Wisely?
*Yin & DNA Yanging, Third Eye*No Eye, Dhammapada.*
"Our Life Is the Creation of Our Mind"
Celebrating being Alive inside a Sequoia forest ~
light effects glistening on a torrential flowing river.
"Liberation is not upset by Happiness or distress"
Consciousness can't remember the past or future,
too frightened to open the curtains for a peak.
Everywhere is good if you have the choice.
Are we falling asleep while we're awake?
"I could Live here, a place called Paradise ~ it's not too quiet."
*20% weight is in its heart * 40 million year old hummingbirds.*

Enter the Palacio Retina

Return of the Angels, Return of the Star Travellers ~
Return of the New Atlantis, Return of New Mayan birds.
Mexican boys picking lettuce in fields at Quetzaltenango
exotic Guatemala girls playing in emerald pools at Tikal.
Fell to Earth from a Sun, tripping on red Stargazer lilies
full of fresh air ~ prana currents, energy, clarity, lucidity.
Lovely colourful auras spinning through your pulsing rhythms

*

Albino Redwoods

"All beings visible & invisible to be liberated in Big Sur"
In the dimension of Real Illusion & 'Psychology' Dr?
Fantastic Brain washing, glorious Brain Worshiping,
stepping out of the physical and mental XXXX box.
Having Microscopic heart surgery in a satellite
not enough chlorophyll, needs a host.
What stops the animals eating it?
Sacred DNA.

*

Civil War Cornucopia before the Tree of Life!

Celebrating a Bastille Day; Nobody wants to be ~
A Slave; who said you were naked in Paradise?
Egalite, fraternite, what's the other one? Eternite!
I think ~ therefore I fell from the tree of Knowledge.
"Life is the Creation of your own Ego-Mind!"
Very difficult for those Master, Slave owners to let go!
Shattered Mirrors of Your Reality; deranging harmony.
Making it Us & Them - Reaction to our Separation
bringing on another disorder, lost in complete Ignorance

*

60/60/24/7/52/365

Cell phone talking in the car,
"Time is Money ~
don't waste a dime"

Don't make the ego such a big deal

It is what it is ~You are as it is, boundlessness, infinity ~
*I Am, if you choose to be the Inspirational light, of Shiva*Shakti.*
Try some life affirming actions, practice Yoga, devotional Bhakti.
Finding your own Inner guru in peaceful grace & generosity.
*Don't worry don't sell your*self for money in too much hurry,*
*don't lose your*self respect or independence; Look beyond*
the dark nightmare enjoy the pleasure of the Cosmic dance.
I love your spontaneously beautiful smile ~ the innocence.
Feeling compassionate, spiritual, natural, social life, being
Human ~ by witnessing your mind & rejecting ego's strife.
Live each moment as if inspired not down in dire denial.

*

"Many go home to the light"

No repression, suppression, oppression, depression, deception;
Agitation of Arthritis, evolution of innumerable 'disorders'
The History of Martyrs and Slaughterers; Who is Whom?
Brainwashing artifice by a London based Oligarch,
"that white baby sucked you dry" spinning Medea.
"You're soldiers, it's your duty to Kill" Obeying orders!
"Slaves of the East India Company have no caste ~
they can be sold & resold by the British Raj!
Break the dominant spell, throw these demons in a cell.
"You dare insult an Officer of the Raj for raping a woman?"
"He who pays decides", new Rules Against everything!
'The Rising Up'

*

We're Living It

*Down loading * Solar distribution, uploading chemical pollution.*
Endangered Mantra Rays in Oceanic colors enlivening our days.
Sonic movements in deep trenches coming to the surface for air ~
Took my honeymoon in Florence, took her to a sacred fountain.
Made a Cosmic journey round to the dark side of the mountain.
"I'm not resisting anymore"

Me & thee, it's Right ~ Paradoxical.
Why denial of your own narcissistic superego ~
denial of yourself and your beautiful relationship?
It's dangerous for you and me; Is it the end of romance, love's fantasy?
Is the idea then to be left with nothing? Just witness your mind in action.
How to take out your wanting, your Personality completely, every
little last bit and then there's unknown Karma from aeons before ~
The designer of your every thought and action which is rational and
*not accustomed to Quantum physics' views from Outer*Inner Space.*
*It's psycho*logical, mental, physical & emotional extra*terrestrial*
entities not knowing much Intuition ~ it's Very dangerous.
Like being stalked by an extinctive Tiger in a panic room,
a virtual Jungle playing inside your mad head in a cloud.
Questioning every move, observing every choice,
reacting to every sense …

*

Can make you Suspicious, superstitious,
give you an introduction to fearful Paranoia
and take you to the Front line of Schizophrenia ~
Lead you down the path to suffering & Intense pain,
despairing, worry, stress, negative depression, denial;
can be very dangerous for the dreamer in your cells Cupid.
Looking for your God in a wilderness can even lead to acts
of Violence, to aggressive demagoguery this mind construct.
A Selfish, greedy, ignorant, cruel personality called humanity.
Inside your heart, to be destroyed by you can be Perilous,
it will take you to the bottom, can make you starve, naked,
be living in sorrow, rejection and failure, having nothing,
given it all up in the hope of truth, lying defeated alone,
under a tree until you broke apart at the end of nothing.
Expected Happiness & feelings of ecstasy are a delusion.
A weakness; Reality itself is an Illusion, very dangerous.
We resonate more living equanimously in the heart...

Or it can break the will of your unique holistic being
and can attack your spirit with hypnotic delirium…
Yet you're led to still believe this is the way of truth,
to Salvation, enlightenment & Holy Grail of Liberation.
You can be broken down like a Crack Addict, a junkie,
you can be self abused, accused, tortured like a 'Godly'
Warrior, Fanatic lost in the grip of a Tyrannical Saviour.
Lost in the 'Righteous Crusade' for Omniscient Power ~
Is it your good Karma to Destroy millions on a battlefield?
Depends on your might this Psycho-Mania for a Holy fight!
Over time you develop a horrible Monster Inside a Cage ~
It can be a devil full of boiling rage ~ in our own environment
with other slaves (captive elves, pixies & fairies)& big beasts!
Pharaohs, Caesars, Generals, dictators, despots, paid Tyrants,
corrupt politicians, false propheteers, popes, predators & priests.
It can be very dangerous, can break you into bits unless disease,
poverty, crime, nano-poisoned food, alienation do it to you first!
Can be dangerous, this belief & faith in Religious thirst ~
this Ignorant brainwashing can be a terrible lasting curse.
You'll have to break your superego isn't that the point of being here?
You'll have absolutely nothing left except yourself, is that what you
are really looking for even though feeling needing, wanting more?
It's a very Powerful, independent choice to take this road
to make this quest there'll be no more unconscious rest ~
Considering breaking your own Mind's self-ego, Id, Identity.
Simply witness it for what it Uniquely is, let it be Cosmically.
Embrace nature's Celebration, embrace your life, open, free,
being here now miraculously for what it is, the master key!
Being humble and content and overjoyed not separatedly.
A part of the living tree ~ in tune with Earth, sky and sea
in touch with all the birds and bees, flowers in harmony.
It can be dangerous, can be a wonderful experience.
Take Your Pick!

Sub Atomic Horus ~ Doing the Business

Looking through tinted windows at Guadalajhara
surrounded by Landscaping of a 'Genprobe Complex'
$ multimillion 'creations', passing a Pet cemetery.
Profit lines of 'black glass temples', Mira Mesa Blvd.
Cloning mothers' chromosomes, looking into future's
mega eyes, living another dream dreaming itself.
"I'm calling about the next wave"
the bird guy, the one with wings

*

At the Gateway to the Heavens

"Your Life is the Creation of Your Mind"
Swimming against the current repressing emotional
pain, wants & fears. Travelling through time & space
travelling with the stars, Intuiting higher intelligence ~
fell into a conceptual, galactic crevasse, facing any anxiety.
They dropped a German Astronaut at the Space Station
made three walks into orbit, spinning 186,000 miles per sec.
Having Incan coffee in the Sputnik café, 150,000 stars above
your head. My wife came from Atlantis' Psychic crystal ball,
passing through blue holographic frontiers of intense radiation.
"We still kiss, lights from inside a Cosmic horizon"
"Attached to my ego in the centre of the Universe"
"Hatred in a Whirlpool on the magma stream of Life!"
"Mindfulness is a direct experience of life, not the concept"

*

*Distant drum * Yin Yanging*

Whatever It's meant to be; She's on her way through
light years on light years of sensational rubbish dumps.
At the intersections of Immeasurable & unfathomable,
*taking the shuttle. Dynamic microscopic * macroscopic.*
In the parking, met a Sufi without his zooming Frisbee.
Changing Polarities & Realities?
Somewhere on a Pacific beach ~

<u>It means something</u>

The most metaphysical but it stopped in your Mind ~
Incomplete, can't feel the movement, change in Time.
Misunderstood the meaning of what it's meant to be ~
Of who I am, of who we are, conveying an inner spirit.
'It's never too late' ~ there's something there, effecting.
Great hope for the future in a house of flying chopsticks!
Let's hope the I Ching thing is right

*

<u>An Alienated Fabergé egg</u>

Elements of Chance, innovative, improvising, in sync...
The Mind of America, the Mind of Modern Persia, Islamic
Republic of Iran in heat; The Mind, Roman Empire in defeat!
*Mind of a practical multi*hemispherical new Chinese dynasty.*
A Mind of 'The Chosen' separated Zion, Holy Isolated, Israel!
The hidden Mind of forbidden Tibet

*

<u>Planet Hemp</u>

Expressions of a Brazilian Survival Cornucopia ~
'Carnival of Apartheid' - the Arrival of Angolan Slaves!
Expensive, commercial, contemporary, lost black rhythm.
Singing Samba, reggae bhajans in Salvador de Bahia.
"Did you ever listen to simply the sound of the World?"
'Bringing the poetic element into the Funk street baile'
All beautiful rhythms, beautiful dancing, beautiful people.
Looking for the Perfect beat ~ mixing, "what do you hear?"
"OK you will find your song"
Didn't want to be 'Knockout Ned' Shot in his head, finale!
Living in shanties, a tough reality ~ 'In Ciadade de Deus.'
Creating Percussion & dance not crazy gang ~ Violence!
Going back to their roots, samba morro, hip hop, reggae,
fusion, funk. Favela not for rich cosmopolitan Bossa Nova.
Blade Runner in the Tropics ~ fuckin with a Volcano Vivo!
Bringing the Revolution, coming from the Source of Life ~

Front Page - One day in the Press - 27/07/2006 LA. Times.
'Residents of the Lebanese Port of Tyre rushed to the site of a multi-storey apartment building said to be the home of a cleric with ties
to Hezbollah which was flattened in an Israeli air strike!
A UN. aid convoy reached the city ~
with a supply of flour and medical kits.'
In Ruins

*

'Camp Victory'
"An officer shoots a boy holding a replica Toy gun....
House to house fighting, dozens of Israeli tanks and
bulldozers backed by missile firing drone aircraft!
Three young children killed including two sisters ~
1400 Rockets, 30 Dead, Israeli shells killed four UN Peacekeepers!
Spider in the web, butterfly in the net regardless of whose nationality.

*

Cross Pollination
Same Cones from different trees
One female seed has to mate with a male seed
carrying all the DNA; creating a Giant Sequoia.
Freezing sunsets ~ Pressing the Panic Button!

*

Kat ^Usher's Pocket Rockets!
"A cease fire opposed by the US. and the British.
That special killing relationship in action again!
If it's not dropping Atomic Bombs, its inhumane
sanctions, indirectly starving one million children!
The city was pummeled, houses razed to the ground.
She resisted the entreaties of nearly all of her European
and Arab counterparts plus the impassioned pleas of ...."
What a Horrible activity Politics is, the way monsters play it!
"The US & UK representatives stood virtually alone in opposing
an Immediate ceasefire haggling over the word
'Immediate'

<u>Militias dismantling their Ford Galaxy</u>

"Eleven Kassam rockets reportedly hit Israel injuring....
Sirens Wailing at the shrine, the US. UK. view prevailed!
Israeli Operation dubbed 'Sampson's Pillars' of corruption.
Incursions targeted orange orchards and olive groves ~
Said to be sites for launching Spuds, rocketing attacks!
50 Tanks & Bulldozers down the center of Shaaf Street.
Against the Wrath of the IDF they are Primitive! "Shalom"
Buzzing of unseen drones overheard ~ "We're not scared!"
Children used to the Idea of death, playing hide and seek.
Sometimes they hit something, sometimes they go backwards.
"We launch them the rest is up to God!"

*

<u>Rare Chinese Shakespeare</u>

Better than 10 Holy Mountains, with hills of tea.
Dali with the surreal hats in forests of glittering snow,
climbing through a Haiku desert, mango sea on LSD.
"It's never too late" changing structures of physics.
So the Spirit's in the trees, Devas inside DNA.
the essence of everything Cosmic

*

<u>E Sense</u>

Not ESSO, EXXON, Non-Sense but Essence.
The 'Real Thing' not Coke but Cones
"I am loving it"
Condition of the Cone ~
not the conditioning of the Coke.
Little wings on seeds detaching and flying away.
American Minds will be opened to other Ideals ~
deceiving the insects to land on them and pollinate.
'Absurd beyond belief'
'Lost in a wilderness of shattered mirrors'
Venus is shining ~ "I believe in the Sun"

A Challenge

Saw marrying you, Love, full desire not 'Terror firma'.
But 'Terra amora' it is ~ for Dhamma seeds to grow!
Oldest tree in the world, the banyan at Anarudhapura.
"Every moment is your teacher" very deep and beautiful.
Plug into it ~ reaching up to the top canopy

*

The Apsara Series

downloading a wet, 3D Vagina ~
Super imposing it with Photoshop,
expressing the essence ~ abstractly.
Kid you came out of one of those trees.
"What are they telling us?" It's Photosynthesis!
These Devas all sitting here on the Ancient Earth.
Long time ~ vibrating energies ~ histories in rings.

*

Hunger Striker

"Saddam Hussein broke his fast, eating bread and fruit
and drinking a can of Coca Cola, a US official said – "
Charges of Mass Murder; Unwarranted citing precedents.
Amazing Product Placement, it must be 'The Real Thing!'

*

"Take the Pain!"

Easy Path this ~ in my memory
It's as if his Mind has left him ~
got rid of all the flawed metaphors…
Good, bad, winners, losers, rights, wrongs, dualities!
Sharing Cosmic Consciousness in a current stream
Vibrating frequencies under the same hot Sun
May all beings be < Free > of Pain > Resonating.
From sensations of hate, desire, Ignorance, suffering.
Don't you see? "Everything is Created in your own Mind"
"May all beings visible and Invisible be ecstatically happy"
And live in Brazil sipping cachaca with a girl from Ipanema.

Artemis In June

Shiva Shakti in a Tree; Is it a Vaginal Vortex, or Cortex?
"Jesus always wants people to give themselves in"
"Saved from the fires of Hell" Pure Monsanto Poisoning!
"You make what you want out of Life ~ your choice"
Relations of a Sensory Overload
Lovely feeling
High energy in the fields.
Purified our lungs
Purified our Minds
Purified our Auras
Spiraling Inspiration

*

*Culture * Fusions*

"Where the most black are the most poor"
'Four million Africans transported to Salvador'
Calling down their Gods of Candomble ~
'Oxun' Angolan Goddess of Love.
Embryos improvising in a ring
Met an erotic, Carioca Priestess dancing Samba,
feeling intensely seduced by her pulsating rhythms

*

Welcome to the Psilocybin Tribe of Light

"You see Pixies on Mushrooms & Aliens on Acid"
*Junkie's Paranoia ~ Withdrawal * A Frozen turkey!*
DT's - then you have to have another line!
No Pranic life in sad phantoms, dead trees.
Being released through Shiva's compassion ~
He's Meditating in the garden of the burning Ghats
"Gives it another rebirth, another chance, changing ~
'Calling a ghost to serve, don't know how to send it back again!'
Transmutation try once more, easy to catch one with Mantras"
Totally pissed off - Who Are You? Ask a psychedelic hippie…

We are on the front line

Test Driving the Acid drops.
We took some Dolphins with us ~
"Too many soldiers not enough Warriors"
"Warriors choose to fight, soldiers are told to".
Making them realise what they could lose!
"We're not physically, mentally aware
that we are Slaves!"

*

In the Belly of a Beast

'School children able to recognise 400 brands by the age ten.
'The Prime Minister demanded the Immediate release
of British hostages from Guantanamo Bay'- "Fuck off!"
'AIR CONDITIONED' Reality; 'Much More the Better.'
Still want Bigger, 'Bigger is the Best' ~ 'Mental Identity'.
Thinking Kyoto is a car made by Dodge in west Virginia.
Nightmares effecting the whole of village Earth, 7 billion
dodgers locked in a battle, Inside Gated communities!
Pechanga Hot Slots, Wendy's old fashioned Hamburgers.
"We're almost there kids" Golden arches sign by Lake Elsinore.
'A Place for Ribs', "We're the Good Guys". Flying to the stars.
No Sizzle, "Listen to Win" Kiss fm. on the 'Uber Empire'
Snap On, snap to it, snap out of it, wake up to the constant bullshit.
You 'Your Life is a creation of the lifelong Conditioning of Your Mind!'
Explorer Discoverer harvesting a Cosmos of growing brains in jars

*

A Smokers' Place

"Such a nice party when everyone is tripping"
"When I walked in everyone
had a chillum in their hand!"
"All the past is wiped out ~
when you are in happiness."
Fifty trips to give out...
"Want some Acid?"

No Rockets coming in today

(25/07/2006 LA.Times) 'The UN post where four Peacekeepers
were Killed by Israeli fire, was hit at least sixteen times over
six hours including five direct hits on the base as its unarmed
staff repeatedly made at least half a dozen calls to top officials
at the Israeli Mission to the UN seeking an end to the attack.'
"Apparently deliberately Targeted" - Deliberately Murdered!
'Additional calls were made to the Israeli Military
by UN Generals on the ground. This is another fascist War Crime!
They went unheeded and fire continued even when a UN rescue
mission was underway after a direct hit on the observer post'
"They were unarmed observers acting in the service of Peace"

*

Spinning Roulette

"Time Is ~ Nothing to do with Money"
Spending Money ~ Spending Time!
** Spending Time together * Wealth.*
Spending Money - Accumulating Money.
Cash Registering ~ your life's Intentions!

*

Smiling

Pleasure of Timeless Space
Not having 1000's of things ~
repeating themselves in my head.

*

Most relaxed guy in town ~ Lost in the Dam!

Matrix's flowing when something is forming due to something else.
Free Love in California with a black Russian in each hand!
Both worked at the Chocolate factory on different shifts...
Unbelievable she was half red Indian DNA; as fit as fuck!
We're the first cloning experiment, couldn't train a local Minotaur.
"I got this love affair with Asia; our Rays made a big impression!"

'Vijnana' ~ thoughtless reality

Rivera's nude, a girl selling Calla & Tiger lilies; Turner's painting light.
Wonderful Sun rising over the ramparts of a ruined Castle in Nepal.
"NASA speculates ~ A Magnet star could erase a credit card's
magnetic strip from over 160,000 kms. away!"
Crab Nebula pulsar, 6000 light years off Earth, rotates 30 times/sec.
X ray telescopes used to harvest the Cosmos for data,
discovering 20 Pulsar Stars in globular clusters.
Tightly bound collections of millions of Stars
Orbiting a Galaxy's rotational center ~ at perihelion.
*Incandescent Spiral, Milky Ways * Supernova tendrils.*
The Visual Poetics of a Noetic Comet Hunter.
What do you want to be when you grow up?
A Mystic

*

*Party Slogan * Corrections*

'You're Safe but you have to do what you're told'
If you have the right connections you're free ~ it's always changing.
"The Knowledge he had was his memory of a Sociopathic Big Brother."
Not satisfactorily under control, go to page (36), press screen to delete!
"Who controls the Present controls the Past,
who Controls the Past Controls the Future ~"
It's all Mind's Phantasmagoria ~ simply be here now

*

'Death Is Not Death'

Dark matter is Real, King Chandragupta ask your Astrologer.
Having no Attachments to the Identification of any Objects.
Vipassana meditation ~ "You have to take it seriously"
I'm more complete, so less ignorance and fear
*of an invisible, energetic * travelling shadow.*
Come back to Your true self
~ to play again

Reality Control took your Independence

The enemy always represented absolute evil, being a Devil.
No agreement is possible, the party could make the past
'Appears as if it never happened' ~You disappeared, sister!
If all the others Accepted the criminal lies the Party Imposed;
If all records told the same tale; delusions passing into History.
'The Ultimate Subtlety' ~ is not so subtle Mein Fuhrer!
"No knowing how much of this legend was True and
how much Invented." Just like what's happenin' today!
'Double thinking' go to page (38), section – para – line -
Inducing consciousness, inducing hypnosis in a paranoiac…
Unconscious you were acting as a subject (slave) of the Realm.
Putting a finger on a definite lie ain't easy in a hostile machine.
Proving nothing with no evidence, brother can you remember?
"A single flicker of the eyes could give you away." (P.39).
Fearful in this confusion keeps you lost in their illusion.
"Don't sweat darling!" With such sophisticated powerfully
computerised machines, today the Matrix is able to know
if you've had any feelings ~ that they've not dictated!

*

The Biology of Belief,

Turning everything you know about the body on its head.
They're the people who want to own & control our World!
What's going on in the cell, where's your super biological Mind?
Before mammals there was a program for this Planet
and we had fuck all to do with it! News from the Front!
This program will continue even if we're here or not.
Every cell is changing whether you want it to or not.
Thoughts and dreams constantly changing
Reconstituting from one to the other ~
Chilling till death, we're the Revolution!
Thank you for your Awesomeness

The Movie of External Existence

Frame by frame could be your next rebirth, slut!
Took a transcendental trip with a chakra ringing
in my zip, found an Indian, Insane, 'Love Affair'.
She's the right way round, "I'm Shiva black relax."
"Your body is your Temple of adoration Lover"
Inviting me in as a friend, keeps it sweet.

*

Rendition Made Legally!

'Hosting' ~ 'A Water boarding Contest.'
US. In terror - gates > could only mean
Suffering under Extreme duress techniques!
Torturing at 'Secret Detention Sites' -'Don't ask - don't answer'
The Authorities don't want to be found out, losing all human credibility!
Your history is only full of wars, murders, exploitation, the devil worship.
Work &/or starve, no Alternatives; "Arbeit machts Frei" - auch nichts gut!

*

The Vatican Hit Squad

How strong is your dedication to stay good?
So much corruption and criminality, selling the water!
You get a lawyer, you're fucked! As Shiva is my Witness.
'You gotta know your rights before you can exercise them'
An old age disease, no it's an accumulation of overriding fears.
Where does radio noise come from, where is the mind plugged in?
"I had six black years." ~ Lying on the floor laughing her head off!
You set a war off in my head and you kept your secret dirty bomb!
"Should I stay or should I go?" Ask your super narcissistic Lover!
Metaphysical massacre ~ Reprogramming yourself to be happy
An Intersectional woman in an unapologetically pink pussy-catsuit.
Filling in at the factories while the men were at War!
'Artists are people sharing their inner beauty'
Who is the most important person in your Life?

Cull Examine

In East Africa the animals run free
if there's a flood, bush fire or famine ~
Lost a million elephants on the plains of Serengeti
Big cats living in boxes flying Economy in the sky
never putting their paws on the ground, left to ~
follow genetic foot prints to an Invisible Planet
A Virtual Zoo for the Noble Sauvage

*

Organ Directly

The Tube from the Source
receive some notion and put it down.
He channeled the Life of Jesus Christ, very nice.
Refurnishing ~ Healing everything with fasting.
Pushin' out the dead brain cells, shifting Maya,
full power metabolism not attached to anything
let the skin absorb Sunshine Prana

*

Purifying blood's imperfections of the body sincerely,
playfully, Krishna's regeneration beside a big river ~
bringing organic, biological food, breathing fresh air,
singing, dancing, celebrating time on the LSD Lotus.
New Year's Party and expressions of Planets flying over
on Astral, magic mushrooms & my first touch of ecstasy
with you Princess

*

Maha Maya Alive

*"They Bomb * Refugee camps"*
An Accidental tourist in Sudan..
Whose suffering with 'Disaster Fatigue' hands up!
Compassion Overload; who develops whom?
Paradise In the Summer
A Tsunami cleared the way for the Mafia!
"It's our responsibility to know it's all a Lie"

Monument Valley
Looking for Time ~
In Space
At the Galaxy Motel
With you
Lying on a sun bed connecting to my Soul
Sweating sisters
*

Shining Bright
Her Heart lit up ~
Like a happy pussy
*

*Erect blue Viagra * Her pink Niagara*
Communicating with a King Cobra in Silence ~
Nice to be accompanied by Your Lover into a Samadhi Tank.
Crawling to you on my heart, petals falling from the sky.
Aphrodite standing in the shell of Immortality
Venus dancing on the tip of my tongue ~
Feeling the breath of a Goddess, the most beautiful
I've ever seen. Caressing her gorgeous arse.
Pulsating, perfect sexual body, gushing ~
"Where are you from?" "Italy"
Masturbating herself on the sunbed,
a show meant only for lucky me.
Beside the languid Arabian sea,
'Grazie mia bellisima Rati.'
Licking you, seducing you, sucking you, entering you.
Kiss me darling, wanting you deeper inside my mouth.
Opening your lusciousness ~ dissolving in my blood stream.
Stop the thoughts, stop thinking, the one I'm searching for Is me.
A lovely, romantic Illusion
*

*Life Fun ** Goa Fun*
Cosmic Romances

*Psycho * Toast*

'Amateur Mycologists searching for the fabled sacred mushroom'
What's Mind-Control all about Professor? Ask a matryoshka doll.
Seeds of the Counter-culture fused in healing, ask any Shaman.
Introducing Fungo Magico not just to get you high Amigo ~
Channelling, calling forth the Spirits in great Abundance.
Ultimately it's a film manifested in this Outer Space-suit
Alchemical reaction, energetic rainbows living in Paradise.
Welcoming the winged Love deities with Cupid Erotes
"I'm not into any orthodoxy at all" ~ I'm a Time traveller.
FREE of EVERYTHING

*

Smoking Black

"All the women stay awake on Ice, speed in Pattaya.
15 Police with Machine guns ~ Waiting for You!
In Dubai 0.0004 gm. stuck to your shoes ~ got Life!
Scrubbing yourself down going through Transit scanners ~
100 gms. in Indonesia, Singapore, Malaysia and they'll Kill You!
½ tolla in his jeans, 'Yabba Yabba do' ~ Not on Your Life!"

*

*Anonymous * Aphorisms*

Don't believe anything ~ Look in the mirror of your heart.
'We are Many they are few, they need us, we don't need them!'
'If it's not us, Who, If it's not now, when?'
'We are living in unprecedented times where the common people finally have
the opportunity to free ourselves from the toxic influence of the ruling class'
Flowers & insects don't have brains flying under the Rainbow's radar,
we can't sense it! "I've neither seen you or touched you in the flesh ~
Into the Love vibe getting tuned into your frequency
Looking for the Cosmic egg in the Brahmanda ~
Singing you lullabies, the 196 sutras of Patanjali

Indian Science Fiction

Sita meditating beside the Lankan Ocean
Battling light & darkness.
Here to provide a Conscious alternative.
A balance ~ to all the shit in this World!
I can survive in India, the Goa tribe,
the rest of the country a Spiritual vibe ~
We can do everything between us ~ meeting
the most amazing people just sitting there
passing the time of day together with a smile.
*'On a divine mission' * lights of a Cosmic Rishi.*
Sadhu walking from Kanya Kumari, Orissa, Vanarasi to Gangotri.
Met indigo children at Auroville, a Yogi Painting at Cholamandel.
*"Hari Rama, Hari Krishna" ~ playing Psy*trance to lovely Radha.*

*

Tsunami Co ordination!

It only made a splash in the city of Pondicherry ~
The Colonial French had built an Impressive Sea wall.
Other's could have done something but that's India!
Making a New Communication Network for Humanity
The sea went out ~
the people went into the sea
collecting dead fish

*

Could have been avoided; Ignorance & Karma.
When you need it you get Super Strength
because it's so Important to you ~ Instinctive!
Full Power no shower 24 hour in a Hurricane

*

Goa Freaks

Less labels, less boxes, less judgments, here now.
*Into a new multi-dimension * the source of Tao.*
Getting rid of Conditioning ~ Mind's distractions
of the ego, here's a chance to Observe, be Alive

A terrible word, 'Squirm'

"All my lemon leaves eaten by caterpillars!"
A herd of cows being chased by a Rottweiler and
running straight towards me! Amber turning into flesh!
"I had that Jekyll and Hyde and it was nasty!"
"I know I was keepin' my Sanity!"
The paranoia, I started to worry…
*Turned into a fly * with the final wash.*
"We don't realise how many jellyfish
are in the Oceans; they call him Flipout!
What do you do with them then?
Try some California Sunshine.
*White Crystal * Clarity*

*

Surya's Sunshine Chip

Satan came on black magic Saturday.
They don't travel without Hanuman ~
On the Metaphysical ship it all makes Sense.
Ways of explaining the unexplainable, to you.
Over the precipice ~ "Italians make the best
Chillums & Charas, Israelis put the Price Up!"
I Love the sea, chilling in a Cosmic lagoon
with Tahitian brides who really adore me!

*

*Magic * Psychic * Deconstruction*

Inspiring children's moments of unlearning
"I'm happy with what I have" put your mind
at ease; I'll take you where you want to go.
A mellow offer no one could refuse, but you ~
Know you want to go, as long as no pain is involved.
Language of Intention ~ Shakti the "I Maker"
Makes Perfect Sense; a horrible Monster like…
A Fascist Army at home anywhere in the World!
Jumping out of this Paradigm into Cosmic wind

Just a Movie Screaming

You want a drama, a thriller, Romantic comedy, tragedy?
A Rainbow, an act of God, not light refracted thru a Prism!
Pure Existence Is In You
Not just what your amazing Brain is Manifesting. And which ~
Hemisphere is being Operated for You & Your achievement?
Right or the left ~ being Creative or Controlled > Organised
10% capacity? What is your Intention? Acting in that vein.
You're a pain ~ in the balls; I took my tent to Lonely beach.
Where the eagles gather, acid made her into an astronaut.
Luminous shape shifting, bouncing back or cracking up?
"America Please Don't Come Here and Help these People!"
flying cups and saucers

*

Get it out

See it as a Time Bomb!
'Doing Business'
With the Aliens shifting black money & gold!
Lookin' at the Talkin' brain-washing Box.
A lie, a lie, after a lie, after another lie..
Focus Your Attention
Clear Your Mind of distractions to feel infinite Space.
Rocket fuel ~ blasting out to the Planet of Dreams.
"I'd turn her loose, go and do your thing"
Having the Energy ~ Awareness
to stand up to the Lawyers, Authorities taking the piss!
The System's Top Conditioners for stating their Values!
Soon you'd hear the Caterpillars start up in the forest,
then the Chainsaws, like someone was being raped!
Trying to find solace in my simple, exploding cocoon.

*

All got different Minds on Free St. ~
You can break it down to Organisms
reaching to the Stars

Ra the God of Light

The Media don't tell you the Obvious ~
If you don't know what's goin' on it's a Mystery
It's a Form of Magic, spells are just the words.
Everything goes back to the breath ~ flowing Love
Before I go I might see something I've never seen before.
That's the Spirit Baba! "I want to taste her oil!"
The Insiders know what's goin' on we're already billions of years old ~
Connecting through each other, extra-sensory perception, Pachamama.
How to heal your mind and body from the pains, torture, rejection, denials?
Dumped in the desert on a freezing night; how to eliminate the treachery?
How to take out the bloody daggers of betrayal from your broken heart?
How to heal your shattered dreams and promises of your trusting Mind?
Overpowering your senses ~You're either critically thinking or a Nazi cunt!
Where's Logos, realising your Mind is creating this full diorama of illusion.
"Know the unknowable merge into impermanent Brahma"

*

Be Liberated ~ from What?

Mobile's microwaves more dangerous than LSD!
We like psychedelic, with a lot of trance ~ in the mix.
Put to the Test in India, "It's there somewhere
but who the fuck knows where?" Very lakhs.
The President of India is a Rocket Scientist.
You mean Missile Science!!! 'Chaos theory'
A nice guy; "Yes I'm a Brain Surgeon too!"
India really does work with fractal Devas of anarchy.
Krishna has all the 64 qualities of Supreme Godhead ~
*(Intelligence) "I like beach life * Love it ~ I like nude vibrations*
of beautifully seductive, very smooth, soft lips smiling at me."

*

Beautiful

What a Smile!

<u>No One Dies Just a Process of Dying</u>

*'The Earth Is a Living Being' ~ multi*dimensional energies…*
It's manna food, on the Level of Inspiration dancing in Space.
Learning how to speak, to Communicate, to feel, to peak.
"I'm Not trying to paint, I'm expressing being with the flow"
She really don't have a clue what she put us through!
'Absolutely Bananas' ~ cool name for a shop.
'To Obey or Not to Obey
To Pay or Not to Pay'
That is the question, if you still really need one!
You're as Free as you want ~ to be, supposedly.
I'm a Sun Worshipper going for bright vital light.
To the Master a lie is the beginning of darkness.
Listening to the whiles of Satan, a seductive Voice.
"Eve come here!" ~ Making every thought captive!

*

<u>Subliminal Syndrome</u>

"Everybody's different
but we expect everybody
to be the same ~"
My lover was afraid of being touched!
She was Hot stuff ~ It's all Maya
I feel like an Angel at the end ~
The life is to change, be here now
"The end of something is always
the beginning of something new"
Nataraj dancing

*

'Life is only a story ~
If you believe it or not'
Having too much Fun #1
In the Vastness of the Land
'Propaganda of another War!'
"I try to Love everyone & so loving myself"

Welcome to (my) Our bed ~ Do What You Like
Gateways into the less density dimension ~
Patterns of the Seed & Flower of Life gyrating, generating.
Remembrance Point ~ Blueprints of all kinds of energy fields.
Sacred Geometry >:< Showing us how to move, it's moving!
(He always saw the Portals spinning at the speed of light)
Misidentifying with the Mass Pain Brain
"Never say no to a spliff!" Natasha....

*

Pineal Wheels
Sent their son to a Psychiatrist.
"Send in the Parents instead!"
"Now about this 3rd eye"
"Spleen absorbs Prana, breaks it down to other charkas"
Undertow ~ Undercurrents against music of the spheres.
A Baby born with the Karma of Herod!

*

Sanskrit Punk Angel
Luma (Moon), Suma * (Queen of the Moon)...
Good negative ions from foam, better Sphere's receptivity.
You get fresh flow ~ Orbs of Tao no more solid structures.
Balance of harmony ~ many beautiful rhythmic dimensions.
'The easy flow the easiest Ride'
Frees all the boundaries to the subconscious realms.
Just Paranoid guided force * Until Centring, tuning in.
Channels, freewheeling, overlapping of the glands.
They build an energy Vortex ^ the etheric body.
Rolled into the joints of an esoteric Master

*

Sweet skin, hypnotic physics, Magic yoga.
How would you ever know that there is a
BOX there; Never Mind ~ that You Live in It!
Going around the sharp edges; If you make it ~
"The road of excess leads to the Palace of Wisdom!"

'Paradise Pharmacy'

'Occult Baba', 'Doctor Estrange', 'Cosmic Bob ~
Still get Leopards on the Prowl in Mumbai's suburbs
Slum dweller taking a piss, Leopard Attack!
A dog fights back, humans are the easiest.
If you break eye contact they'll leap on you.
If you come across a Leopard
Make Loud noises, throw your arms about
If that don't work
Forget it

*

Republic Under the Carpet!

Full of Bananas all over Incredible India (And the rest)!
Lots of toxic Bananas in the modern, corrupt Indian Democracy ~
As many Bananas as on top of Carmen Miranda's wiggling head!
The Indian Justice System has lots of expensive, overripe Bananas.
Most people living in Indian Villages swallow dal & rice & Bananas.
Traditionally growing nothing but Bananas, only knowing Bananas.
And what do they have in common with Honduras? Bent Bananas!
You can get away with Rape, Murder & Killing with their Bananas?

*

Toxic Rich, He knows the Planet

Will you dance with Charley Chang ~
Will you dance with six-armed Nataraj?
Let the Universe Roll ~ Let Maya play out her role
On a higher Level ~ You have many sacred hearts.
*Came from Venus' Energy * knocking at Your door!*
"It's amazing you haven't had a nervous breakdown"
Creating your Own Matrix, creating your Spiritual field!
Manifesting the challenge, witnessing Mind's mime.
*Always come back to the center * Out of the storm.*
Coming from the open, honest, true heart Please ~
"Give me a ticket to the nearest place by the sea!"
Took her kids to the refuge center in Devon ~

Inalienable Natural Laws & Rights

They didn't just come out of caves and think, let's build a Pyramid!
Wiped out all our memories of Gondwanaland ~ still in Shock!
Where do we live? We live somewhere in a Space in your head.
We were born into Slavery, I didn't even know it, you were sold!
Got a Birth-Certificate ~ Organic life growing in a sunlit pond.
On the cusp of energetic exchange & stuff inter-mingling.
They made us all slaves, said we were dead, didn't exist
Until we woke up and asked for our Cosmic given rights.
We are Living men & women; walked out, case dismissed.

*

Party

We called him lucky Pierre.
Wanted to score, took a Pill
*Invitation to a Psyber*Solstice.*
"Follow that Police helicopter"
Looking for Aussie dread lockers
Giving out Roses
Ready to perceive & receive them.

*

I'm Pilling

"And I'm as cheap as you like" on the Love Train.
"3rd eye opener ~ I love big, spacious, open cabins"
"You'll have to go to Capetown, for the colours!"
Gushin' let's have it for the young Goddesses of Love.
"I haven't done enough tripping, sounds crazy.
Magic in the Words, send in the horniest Satyrs!
You have a lot of affinity with the pussy ~ willow.
Pretty intense, chopped the head off his wife's lover!
Lascivious fauns attending Dionysus and his maenads.
Picking them up without getting their machetes out.
Check yourself boy, who you think you're talkin' to?

Photosynthesis Not Photoshop

Finding the Time ~ to do it all & still smile.
One with everything, seizing the moment
She loves Pune contrasts and I love her.
Met together on Mahatma Gandhi Road.
We should flash it ~ all the time, lightning!
Simple equation, no complication that rhymes
Accept it for what it is ~ essence in an oak tree of life.
The West is never fulfilled always striving, to get more.
It's natural law, natural high, natural flaw, natural sky
natural awareness, natural magnetic Solar light
natural owl flying through a black moon night
*extra sensory perception * Priya Is Loved*

*

Beams

Librettists don't talk Bollocks, bing, bang bosh!
Your Choice? Free will to chill or thrill.
Give the Info; to decide for themselves
not your responsibility, spirit of the lamb,
taste buds of a slave ~ over the Ocean
night lights reflecting in its eyes

*

Might have the bollocks, but he's forgotten
what they're for and doesn't know what day it is!
If the Vessels full of shit, you only talk shit.
Guilty of sedition in the back alleys of Venice.
'The Priest playing a Violin in a Brothel'
Who wrote Political Poems subversive of the Enlightenment?
His lover was condemned by an anonymous denunciation!
Crystallised the themes of ~ 'A marriage made in Heaven'.
*One dimensional * three dimensional lives related to yours.*
"I wasn't looking for it ~ It found me!"
"You must meet the Emperor"

Molten Lava

"God wills what will happen or not happens"
Healthier is Happier;
High, higher Vibration
Harmony ~ In tune, on the Shiva moon.
He was negative & depressed
needing healing on the beach in Goa.
My head's so sweet
In front of my face embracing the Imperfections.
"Ask not what your Planet can do for you
Ask what you can do for your Planet"
'Mother Nature's selfless gift of life'
It took seven years of Research ~
to discover 'Derma Genesis' at L'Oreal.
"You're definitely Not worth it to her, next!"

*

Electronic footprint 'hard stop' on your chest/brain.
Living in a culture, society, system, country, family
of Permanent, domestic violence, sleeping with insane
clenched fists and a media's frenzy, in your home town.
Unrequited neurotic, super egoist, narcissist in denial; Exact!
Lost ~ Gone forever, your heart Wants to Scream & Scream!
Living beyond those rules, regs; controls, morals, laws
We're being spied on, tracked by CCTV, data monitored.
Global small cameras put in walls (inside false eyelashes)
Biometrics, Iris' recognition of your loss of privacy, 'Uh!'
"If you got nothing to hide you got nothing to worry about"
Where did I hear that before, Crown Prosecution Service?
SO19, Special Police Firearms Unit, claimed self defence,
they shot 7 times an unarmed, innocent Man; by mistake!
The Independent Police Complaints Commission forced no
RESIGNATIONS

*

Happiness <> Monopoly

'Like a Pig in shit' roasted them with ergot in fiery Salem.
Government Mafia got you over a barrel of global taxes.
'There would be no more suffering lay down the burden.'
Death, "Mozart ended up a man in an Unmarked grave!"
Head of Counter Terrorism becomes a Witchfinder - General.
Guilty by Association, brother in a Red Mosque or shop kiosk?
'Assumed guilty before proven Innocent.' Show us what you got!"
Why not a test of fire or water, remember those times?
Radiant denouement; Please forgive me, 'habeas corpus'
The dignity of servants as human beings in a feudal time ~
If you grow up listening to war every day, hearing hearts crying;
"Poetry is the door to music" & doors to oppression or freedom?
Now let's all sing the Hymn, 'Ius primus noces'

*

Manipulating Shares in Apple Pie

Performing Americans with Global Elites ~ (Bilderbuggered!)
Class War from above; Demanding higher profits of Greed.
Aug. 22/2007 started a Bull Market running through the street.
Commercial Oligarchies living in the city with security Walls.
Booming Management doing anything to keep wages down!
Living on Peanuts, not a myth of Nickel & dime workings.
Wearing a name Tag on your chest, 'No Free Lunches'
And No Free Time < in return
Living on a Line > of Credit.
Supplying & Demanding; what comforts for these Riches?
Laws of Nature, Laws of Economics, Corruption of Greed.
What about 75% of humanity in this World in direst need?
USA the biggest exporter of Capitalism overseas, UK no.2
Who owns the Yankees, who are these Invisible Predators?
Which 'Vested Interests' from the Middle East to China
who are 'The Middle Men' with an Abundance of serfs?
*Changing Ignorance * Kali Yuga is 'In a Perpetual War.'*
A Reality Check ~ Money Makes the World Go round?

Don't be too serious
Let them get on with it ~ ride it out!
"You gotta stick your tongue right in it"
Mr. Psyche delicious
'Right Attitude'
Why not?
I Gave Up ~ Sweet Surrender.
"Can't fight with the whole"
Swimming upstream ~
Lucky You
"I only care about Myself"
"You are the only one!"
Reflections ~ Tuning In
'It's not me ~ or you'
On an Island in the Gulf stream
"Have to be free to Love ~
can only Love if you are free"
Ayurvedic violet blue flame's destiny
Already extra sensitive enough without it!
A Mover ~ dancing Shiva around his neck.
Captain Methrie Shanty on a Sputnik Excursion!
Flying on a Psychedelic troika with a high Speed-
Impediment ~ waiting for the Alphonse mangoes.
Came home she was sitting on the balcony...
Rainbow Open Fire Circle
Praying, oming ~ making trance music.
"We are already enlightened but unaware of it"
Hard diamonds to swallow with slaves down the mine.
My friend has a very nice, vulcanised Yoni YoYo on a string.
"I like Paradise ~ Paradise in Your Natural Self"
The Sun is Liberated, the radiant one
the Jewel in the sky.
No rotten apples or fig leaves ~

Travel Lightly

Everyone's got baggage ~
She's a mess in my mind!
If you don't go on Ritalin
You don't go to the crèche.
"Depression is anger
turned inwards ~
nobody gives a fuck!
Looking for 'sympathy'?
'It's between shit and syphilis,
in the uncompassionate dictionary.
Smiling faces of the Easter Island giants.
....didn't see it comin

*

Paradise Is What You Make It

"It's dangerous taking powders!"
They don't know how to handle them ~
& their women, their drugs, their stupid behavior!
As long as you identify with the 'I AM' there is Ego.
There is No 'I AM' ... there is No Ego, No You ~
If YOU don't exist you become One with God.
I see the Sun coming up inside you.

*

Letting it go Unconditionally.

How can I judge things in my conceptualised consciousness?
Just sees the Things! Everyone has a different perspective.
A learning curve ~ having a conversation with a kid.
When I get that I will find myself.
The new luxury Mercedes, but are they happy?
They never find themselves, where to find yourself?
If you wanna be an Angel. A what? A hell's Angel!
Psychedelic is more than surreal.

*Mother Arctic's * Exquisite Lights*

"Going for the Burn" ~ at 54,000 miles per hour!
We must make it happen, powering down the craft.
Inside Your wet Lunar module, sweating Prototype ~
Romantic, flying with a delicious Cosmonaut of Venus
Coming down the Magnetic superhighways of her Sun.
*Energetic Powers * Climaxes firing into Aurora's Borealis.*
Writhing wildest spaces

*

Strict Laws

"Houston 500 we have had a problem"
Playing both sides against the Middle ~
Dangerous, an impending mega disaster!
Caligula XXXX Improvising at the Alamo.
The Rules for Consensual Adults in Texas.
OK cowboy ~ welcome to the 21st Century!
$40 for a nude Fantasy room, stay 3 feet apart!

*

'Cosmic Energy Conduits' (Independent. 13/12/2007)

She came through Space to my azure, Crystal Island
*Roman Goddess of Dawn * Greek Goddess of Wind.*
Travelling from the Sun to Earth; NASA's; 'Themis' ~
A fleet of 5 micro Satellites > Visualising the Magnetic 3D.
Structure/Invisible Superhighways twisting Magnetic fields ~
As wide as Earth, forming, unraveling in seconds. 40,000 miles above
*Earth*Magnetopause*Solar wind Particles flowing in these Channels,*
meeting magnetic fields of Earth's upper atmosphere; colliding with
excited electrons spinning inside atoms of the molecules of gases ~
transmuting to a higher energy state. Then cooling to its lower energy
state, we get the colours, energies of geomagnetic storms, Auroras.
Triggering, emitting visible (Northern) lights <> Total energy
of this two hour event is 500,000 billion joules ~
equivalent energy to make a 5.5 earthquake

Orpheus' Night
Centered In the Mirror
Looking at My Mind ~
Looking Into My Mind…
I'm not a Slave anymore!
*Deepening * Visibility*
of the colours of the light
*

Splish Splash Splosh
Anxiety Attacks Inside the Mothership.
No Power for the Guidance systems ~
No Navigation, missing the home Planet.
Rising up, Aligning with your Cusp ~
brought me back from the brink of disaster,
back for reentry into you darling.
Seeing your heart beating in the heat
50,000 pieces through a telescope lens.
Drifting in the infinite ocean into your arms.
Inside the perfect gravity of an Aquarian capsule.
Powerless in the Space lifeboat, blackout time.
Nothing we could do counting down to Zero
sharing moments of elation ~
ending of a Nightmare
*

Recovering Shanti Art
Not for everyone, swimming on top of Stingrays
or Live baiting Cobras & Rattlesnakes; Whew!
A Monster Crocodile attacking a pride of Lions!
An Almost Certain Catastrophe ~
should have heard from the crew.
Surviving or not surviving
giving pain for pain
'I'm going Mad'
Lost In Space

Show Trials *(Nov 5th /2007 Sunday Times)*
"At the beginning of the Iraq war in March 2003. Britain dropped
100,000 cluster bombs. They were also used in Kosovo
And by Israeli forces in Lebanon in the summer of 2005!
Hilary Benn claimed that Cluster munitions are "essentially
equivalent to Land Mines. The bomblets frequently ~
fail to detonate leaving a deadly trap for any passersby"
"It is difficult then to see how we can hold so prominent
a position against land mines yet somehow continue ~
to advocate that the use of Cluster bombs is acceptable"

*

The Dye Is Cast Continuously ~ Finding the Balance
Life is Prana if you haven't got breath forget it, 'Kaput!'
Until the so called last one; critical each breath, Now ~
Pain Killer calming, darling, Serotonin's all over the place.
Caffeine withdrawals and sugar ~ the Real Shocker!
The Brain doesn't like it, any change ~ readjusting to
old habits, flying through, crawling to the Safety Zone,
breaking rusty, bolted barriers to the edgy, holy rogue.
Mind's raison d'etre, limitation is exactly that ~ Limit only to
Ideas & FORMS. "He was a Hippie" 80 Pills a week diversity!
In a tunnel watching a white light ~ I was gone.
She's fuelled us up, ready for more!
Who cares anyway, she's still goin'
The first time ~ full of beauty

*

That African Drum Personality!
Flowing multi#dimensionality ~ Congo rivers!
Finally out of his terrible pain, my friend...
Trance dancing with the legs crossed Baba.
Orchids and a Lotus in deep water
THIS IS BEAUTIFUL
Floating with Venus

See the Cossack Dancers!

The +ve side of drugs; do you need some MDMA?
Balancing on top of hallucinations ^ trip not tripping
*Progress of the experience itself, not Judge*mental.*
Liberation of the quality of a moment ~ being here now.
"Turn the other cheek", Jesus said, it's up to you!
Who Knows, who you're goin' to meet ~ on a river bend?
Completely abstract synergy, it's filigree woven into Reality ~
Another dimension, I recognise that Fear; 'Cool & groovy dear'
To be Open to whatever comes ~ Walkin' the Walk.
"I was gutted".. went off to explore sacred mantras

*

Insatiable Realms

Mind-Form is only Conceptual ~
Follow your Heart's own Language.
Getting on the wrong bus, in the wrong direction.
Nice to have balance ~ "Do you need help?"
Sanskrit Guru, 'Out of darkness into the light'
Going in the jet or the bullock cart, full on ignorance!
Only so many breaths ~ little sperm & organic eggs.
Individuals are Oppressed, a bit twitchy ~ I got Mine.

*

Rappin' Rockin' at every Sun settin' ~
They say her kitchen was Crack Central.
Cock for Rock, glass dicks all over the place,
got her hooked, ½ ton of Charley, Coke Crow!
"It's not about the Perfection it's about the moment"
"I'm not at Liberty to say" ~ A bitter sweet life.
"Love can't be erased".. next to Heaven sent.
Hitch hiking on stumps to the Moon; a Manic Panic!
Money speaks for Democracy. 'Come Jump to the front
of the longest Queue; corrupt bureaucracy at its worst!'
Yeah, that's another load off my Mind.
Beep, "You have no new messages ..."

UK. Gambling Net

Punters can have a flutter
using up to two Credit Cards!
I'm playing Devil's Advocate
The Draconian Social School
full of five armed bandits, bling bling!
Know the Rules, don't get a Ticket ~
(with her things) she's vanished forever...
"You'll always be Mine" ~ What a Madness!
A Slave Addicted to Possession-Obsession.
Lost every last sense

*

Island's White Teepee Myth

feeding the worms
Up for it, always a smile on the face.
"I'm Home", as if it's got a will of its own.
A step in the right direction
An Alien form inside, unbelievable water ~ ask Emoto.
*Apsara's perfect beauty * Andaman Island's sun rising,*
that's what's called Global Warming, my toes in the surf!
Symphonies of blues, turquoise and magenta hot angel lips.
Besotted, Alarm Bells ringing ~
Give me Liberation of any sort!
"They invented marriage because divorce is so good"
Your very emotional future!

*

Desiring Incompatible damsel in the high Castle Tower,
running through the wild streets of a Dark Carnival!
Whatever you Feel is Real ~ Who needs a Brain?
"Peace is more important than Love but when you
have True Peace you have Love"
Good or bad, why not good & bad or good & better forever?
Under control no possession no obsession no expectation.
'Perfect by Itself * Perfect in Itself'

Trappings of Mind

*Focusing * just a method of going Inside.*
No branding, just essential point of breath ~
Got the Force, living within a golden Magus.
Why waste your time attacking a fiery bush,
"Love thy neighbour" ~ could that be true?
At Peace with ourselves, own Peaceful Vibe.

*

Rabelais' Perfect Iris
Another Goddess
She sent Shivas
down my spine
Tickling strange little blue men & 'putto' cherubim.
We'll see we'll see, there's more to the big picture
than meets the cortex, ask any envious Viking.
DNA. clinging to the mast of grim Odin,
lost in a Maelstrom of axes & arrows.
Is this what you call 'Civilisation' mate?
Feeding your children alive to vultures
in the middle of the Slave market

*

Why you wearing a shirt so short?
I can read your iridescent, luscious lips,
created like Aphrodite's voluptuous hips.
Daddy come to church, need some saving!
Azul Govinda's 16,000 wives & one girlfriend;
we've got it back to front, the wrong way round.
Candy flipping in Lhasa with a talking rainbow,
key to Doors of Psychoactive designs. Ask the Oracle.
Didn't I see you at the Maharajah's Palace in Jaipur?
Healing, channeling, ask upstairs; It's all about Trust.
Waiting for the farmer to pull me out of the field. Thanks.
Rooted in the Mind >:< Thinking >:< Entrapment, Escape!
Magic Angels showering you with Love ~ full Enchantment

'Capitalism'

'The Sun never set on the British Empire'
A freak of Nature!
Where Nothing is Sacred

*

You being Clear

Where there's mountains there's usually a river.
Giving Qi Gong energy to the Good Stuff ~
don't give Any energy to the bad Stuff.
Let it run (its self) out ~
It gets better; Oh Really!
*Out on a Star * Cloud #9*

*

Sacred Olives

How old Are You?
As old as the Universe
As old as each other ~
always to give something, born with no Time.
So Full on, bring It on! "Show me what you got!"
What does your experience tell you ~ Sweetheart?
It Stops You ~ resistances, as soon as you Stop.
Don't be Scared ~ "If You Stop You Die."
Love with Freedom, "very nice to meet you"

*

Freedom Atoms fizzing; a very Healthy Independence ~
Doing the Best you could, looking yourself in the mirror ~
Seductive, chilled men not Frankensteins in scarlet! let go Ego.
Sorry got a Big erection; my moist vagina's reacting to a wet, hot,
damp monsoon season, to a full Moon blowing sultry Typhoons!
Conditioning is always there, so it's difficult to be self-aware.
True near Impossible to let go ~ flow; Be Realistic mate,
who can switch off the desires of a lifetime's DNA. fires?
Programmed from when I saw Prehistoric Raquel Welch
screaming sex, sucking a bone in fur

Oreibi ~ I like my natural life!
Impossible to be detached in a marriage, good luck mate ~
As soon as they lived together, they began to hate each other.
Everyone needs their own space, a totally balanced centre!
'People have this achieving stuff too strong
And they don't know how to let it go ~
Conditioning the Conditioned
It's all about Me
And we want to
Live Our Lives
Together ~
Your own Spaces
And own Lives
being together
because you want
to be together &
Celebrate Life
*

Squeeze It
'Related to Slaves, stolen from Africa and beyond'
"My dad eats the eyeballs of a goat ~ Raw!"
'What doesn't kill you will make you stronger'
"We're more Powerful than God!"
"Make Contact * Keep Waving"
"You're already on their blacklist,
they will come for you for sure!"
She's touching all the elements...
'Every experience we have is part of that ~
understanding even if we don't understand it'
The mind doesn't die with death....
It follows you until you transcend
Then you will be worshipped.

<u>Another New Age</u>

Weak at the Knees, tone,
communicating with dogs,
walking past Slashers.
Fear clouds
Your Substance
Eliminate it
It's Nothing but the Mind.
Being No Mind ~
If fear comes Up often,
grab it by the nuts!
Push on through (that Pain)
Face it, become more Confident
I've done a few Stupid things ~
Aware of fear
Dogs can smell it ~
Strong Bush Instincts
they're vory handy.
Put animals on Heart attack patients
Sit a dog on your lap &
You're going more down to Earth.
Helps to Ground us ~
'From a nice piece of Deception'
Who made your God figure mate?
Dog Chakra, vibrating of a dog's head.
Good sleeping on a woman's stomach.
My Crown Chakra on her Yoni Chakra
The old curse, the old Cure for sure ~
Women can be really good at screaming,
healing, can make a lot of Peace & pleasure
(with their Goddess sitting on your Kamachakra)
Fig. of 8's ~ flooded tantra, spiraling Kundalinis.
Entwined (physical bodies) & Energies' Vortices.
Connection to the leaping Violet flames ~

Mapped the Whole System
"Four microdots & a Velvet Blindfold"
Face to face with the Visions of a spinning Pineal Chakra.
Magnetic resonance smashed in through your window.
The hawk flew out and landed on a diamond Pyramid.
Visualized the crystals to heal your 'Energy chords'
Any bad blood relationships, horrible environments?
Keeping them clean with the Power
Taking hold of 'The Hands of Light'

*

Healing the Crack
Not Visible but Physical ~
entity having an Aura massage.
Clearing your energy with Chi Qong
Waving your arms,
getting rid of the dust.
They get the Vibe ~
Prevention of things happening
for the future, things you See
that Plague Your Mind

*

Tao channeling energy, moving your own energy
around the body ~ electromagnetic pulses
so it doesn't get blocked ~ Rediverting
nerves, Infectious disease vibrations.
Acupuncture a very simple Art
Doing Open Heart Surgery on my exquisite Lover.
Later opening the brain of a hairy Monster!
"It Rings True ~
It's Real for You"
Enzymes on the end of your finger
digging the earth, touching a carrot.
Don't sweep the details Underground.
"What is there to regret, for digestion?"

Oberon, 'A Green Light has turned Up'.
Thought was to train a more or less conventional Brain.
Idea to get over the fear of it ~
Believing You have enough room.
Storing pain ~ all over the body,
nerves dancing in every atom
getting Mind to grow ~ flow
through your whole Energetic aura.
A sponge full of Quantum water ~
Why not stretch Your Mind throughout
Your field of sense conditioning...
all over feeling of Mindfulness aglow?
Feel what's going on round you, in you.
Minds communicating, living as a witness ~
Uncovered Pineal gland of a reptile, Insight Inside.
Closer to Instinct, reactive as well as hell.
First early warning system

*

Just a Symptom of her Synapses
Inner Guru's Mind free, didn't need trips, already there!
The Masai are running 100 kms without stopping ~
to drink blood. It was a good injury, more in the mind.
The Babas in India say from Time to Time
"A good hit on the head is good for you"
The person who invented money, just piss on it.
My job is moving stones across the Planet.
*Psychic*Awareness, realigning the Landscape ~*
Electronic, Solar energy from the Sun's fires raging!
Magnetic resonances swimming in little green Rocks.
"It's not the drugs; really it's the processor acting it out"
'Take a drug and control it or take a drug let it control you'
or simply be ~ without any bars is being in the sacred now.
How deep is deep in the trenches of Fault lines?

'Lawful Rebellion'

Governmental and legal mass deception!
The judge won't trespass on your rights.
He swore an oath to uphold them. Tie her up!
The deep fix is everywhere, a million spider webs.
You're standing in the dock because of your consent.
What jurisdiction have you got over me? Who are you?
Your God given rights! What crime has been committed?
Arresting you as Unknown

*

Micro-dosing Chocolate Vapour!

When the bubbles are done it's ready, don't make it too thick ~
"I read Alice in Wonderland in crack rehab; that's where I met my first wife.
IQ; Intelligence is based on the Test's parameters, that is measuring it!
*De*toxing is hip, tell them that at FUKUSHIMA; Pachamama poisoners.*
The World Governments and Global media have said nothing…
Just like with Chemtrails, HAARP or Crimes Against the Planet!

*

Surrendering Obsessional Cigarette

Always needing to be in Control ~
Negative Ions in the air, in your hair.
Such a Shame to always complain
Such a Shame, this Habit to blame
Such a Shame to receive this Pain,
they don't even realise they're doing it!
It's horrible, why do they do it?
No space or patience for others

*

Eton's Comedy Class of Errors

'The 1st WW' was Hell on Earth'
Welcome to the 'Brave New World'
People Made to Order in Hatcheries.
Reserved by the upper caste

<u>"Over to You"</u>

Higher frequencies bathing in your heart ~
Wanna go for a ride on my battlecat and get an easter egg?
"I'm just lookin for an Angel, with a virtual creamchoc clit"
"& I'm just lookin' for a heartbeat .... a pulse!"
A mobile vibrator, "coming when you want!"

*

<u>Living in Tunnel Vision</u>

Where you gonna go?
*You can only go Inside your*self ~*
Otherwise you're always on the run.
What to do?
You can always be Present
Internally stepping beyond.
What's happening?
Connecting with that eternal Space.
"I gotta live somewhere"
You are living here now
You can only see impermanence from permanence
You can only see permanence from impermanence ~
the idea of duality. "I'm the Present in the Present"
'ALL TIME'S RELATIVE DIMENSIONS IN SPACE'
Aborigines hiding crystal goannas from Atlantis; How?
People think they know.

*

<u>We're All Masters</u>

'Severe lack of Interest Syndrome'
To free ourselves ~ No Tracks.
End the concept of Duality
Separation is the first lie,
challenging Shanti Tantra!
*It's beautiful Inside * Outside*
*Inter*net mingling on the highest planes ~*
with a gorgeous Etruscan model of Raphael

Celestial Navigation

Sleeping on a 500 Pyramid ^^^ cosy mattress.
Talking to a dead man ~ going out of his body.
Operating for 5 days, rebuilding energy systems.
What's more Important ~ than Life?
One lick and you're gone ~ Relationships.
"I like to go the simple and easy way"
No you don't have any brakes!
No rules, paralysed on the ground
"I got it figured out"
In my chest I hear ~ Angels singing.
He always had to talk to the Divine.
Pain ~ "I'm Alive!"
Full bore on my Suzuki Samurai.
Brought me back to the top…

*

'Hotel Earth'

Life is a holiday, you come and go ~
Impermanence ~ of Universal waves.
The only place - left to go Inside
When the Polar caps melt and flood.
The Eternal force of Life, will Manifest,
talking to the Humpbacks > Level 55.
Communicating over 1000's of miles, telling their young ~
"To stay out of these waters, they're extinctly dangerous".
Rates of curiosity and senses of play ~ when humans absent.
Dolphins mean good sashimi to a Japanese (1/6 of fish stock!)
How much grain to grow a genetic cow to it being butchered?
Now all gone into Ethanol to run your 4WD car, not animal feed.
The Worst Place in the World to be Poor, no Prime US -
Grateful for what they have as a successful definition of a Society,
not with a Concentration camp from Hell, and dosed up to the max,
wearing Fluor-orange, jump suits! What is Quality of Enlightenment?
A total hunting, beautiful, metallic green spider jumping ~

'Karunish' (Sanskrit for Compassion)
Aware of Amazonia's fecund Kundalini ~
Taking lessons from Khajuraho's frequency.
Practicing Tantra mantra tantra Prana
try it with your special #1 Goddess.
Serpent power (coming) into psychic shower.
Identity of essence, you know how to use it?
'Enlightenment' ~ I don't like that Word anymore.
I'm not advocating drugs, certainly not any addictions.
I'm advocating free Consciousness ~ with a smile inside.
Then you figure it out; like what about just observing Mind?
Othello's tears for lovely Desdemona's untimely departure!
Found yourself disoriented, looking for Brindavan,
looking for protection sailing in a crystal dhow ~
A full on session purifying your mind.
Vibrating in waves arriving at the Brahma Vihara.
Channeling the Love of music in your eyes

*

Inside 88888888 Outside
Soma walking through Amritsar in the smoky, dusky haze ~
listening to the chanting from shimmering Golden Temples.
Saw Greek Meniskos rising over Mughal domes ablaze.
Astral friendship releasing the dramas of energy storms.
Living naturally, freely in the Sun beside ancient stones,
watching an (exquisite) beauty contest in classical Harrapa

*

Reiki Lettuce
A tattoo that said it had kept him alive or it could be a sign
of his death in Iran! "I love the juice", in a German accent.
Entering a Haiku competition, having to invoke a season.
'I thought he'd died in captivity, bastard! Another dark winter'
Intuitive 'Camoes' at a jet propulsion Laboratory & Giant
Radio telescopes receiving; crosses from deepest Space.
Gems of leaves rustling in the Autumn breeze, light showers.

What to say!

*Free association * surreal elements, imaginary dreams.*
Shadows in glinting emeralds of giant green panoplies,
holding a billion invisible species of Devas and Apsaras.
IDEA. and you want to cut it down for minimal Furniture!
Wonder worms with eyes fixed on escape, exploding,
picking violet meteorites from your starlit hair.

*

Gathering at a Lovers' festival, building a Pyre of hearts,
sprinkling with fresh mangoes, luscious fruit & mantras.
Living in the grass with my angel, smiling on her back.

*

Samurai without Visas

Disheartening, flashing chaos racing in burning Rickshaws.
Baby frogs turning into the sperm of soulless mercenaries.
Anymore fragments of anxiety found in Kyoto's canals?
Enough opium drops rolling off the tongue for everyone.
Listening to the wind, birds & elephants on the rumbling.
Tough, OK with the Pain, a friendship of Mother Nature,
before you go I'd like to suck your purple lips again ~
"Go and sit on a hill and let the air heal it"
Whatever's going on in the moment it's all connected.
She stepped through me into her liquid destiny

*

The Best is The Best

Sensed it, yearning for you ~ addicted to your image!
Patterns of eternity shining on your summer blouse.
Within a billion cells of my being fully aroused.
"The Masala chai is strong today"
Mangoes raining down from the sky…
Depends on myself, my Open Mind; being Kind.
Listening to your Celestial heartbeat on my chest ~
"Utopia or oblivion? Since the Weapon proceeds Mankind,
did Mankind evolve strictly for the use of it?"

Cold Diamond Ego

He's in charge, 'the Man' a poor Zealot.
Can hear the Taliban cheering in Bamyan valley!
He Loves to be Unconscious, Consummated.
Riding to Victory; needs to chop his head off!
Had a nervous breakdown; waiting for you to come.
Instinct straight to the Point; how is his heart?
"Hitler would pat her hair, a platonic relationship!"
"You're choking me!" "I just love you!"
What's your feeling at the end of the day?
Life and death kisses

*

'Che Sera Sera'

Riding in a troika; how you can free flow ~
with lots of money, with lots of honey
getting in fine tune ~ with My Self.
Adjusting the frequencies
maybe we always had it ~
just developed it ~ whatever is.
Hanuman's Celestial number.
Reincarnation of Rama & Sita
Shiva Parvati, Vishnu Laxmi.
Step into that moment ~
What is meant to be,
will happen, "No more Control"
Ripples in pools of Serotonin ~
Tribal beat on a Planet out in Space
everyone gone, back to Pachamama.
Sometimes things are better forgotten
at some level flowing with the Cosmic Stars
Between Immense Oceans of extremes ~
Forgetting it or remembering it, dreamtime.
Why Any of It?
Be In THIS Moment

<u>Being Very Happy</u>

Why would you do that to Yourself
Don't You want to be ~ happy?
Realising a lot to do with Planet Goa.
Diving it's not competitive, you have a buddy.
Instinctively looking out for each other ~
Peaceful World out on a Cruise (Missile)
Illuminating a Royal fuck-up!
I paint for the Universe
Very fine lines, sometimes I trip over the edge.
"If you can't see through this shit...
You deserve to be the tool that you are".
You have to be fit to Live in India, can't pretend...
India makes you fit to be alive or you die my friend.
This Is Full Respect

*

*<u>Thank You * Thank You</u>*

We dream a lot, is that a 'Time-Space Quake'?
We all come from a Cosmic energy milkshake.
True Intention that you can heal yourself,
making it up as I go along (in my heart).
You'd accept your part in it ~ naturally.
There's always someone in there to take
advantage, exploit & Control other people!
"Hey Buddy You can have one for free"
Prisms Implanted from the NSA, not Gaia.
They only ask ~ for your Soul.
Some sort of dark, covert Manifest.
A Plan for Controlling all the World.
Their Plan is Working, no free will!
Mathematics put People on the Moon.
Embrace No TV, smart phone, media for a whole month,
And watch everywhere how the World Changes.
"I'm putting Full Power Into the Healing"

*Travelling * together through Time * Space*
Estimation of your friend & enemies.
You ladies want to go to the Circus?
"Became rich by Helping people…
There's nothing Wrong with being Rich
but being Selfish"

*

I would say this Resistance; barrier, this barricade
'Is the Mind' - Oui, Mon General? Certainement!
The Key is to just go through Space M. Rimbaud ~
& enjoy 'La belle Chateau de notre mère', M.Pagnol,
& exquisite deconstruction of une folle 'femme fatale'
Sig. Picasso & go with surreal abstract flow Sig. Miro.
Mind Is the Lock to Space, need a key to open destiny
or maybe not if there is No door or walls of separation.

*

Simple is clarity, don't want to give any sense of guilty.
I said to her, "to do whatever you want just be Happy"
It's up to us to make Ourselves happy And realized ~
Understanding, doing it for each other, just being.
You have to know how to say 'No'. To be a sailor ~
on your ship not expecting, making a vow, attaching
happiness to anyone or anything anymore, is easy ~
How difficult it can be surfing through wide open seas.
*Keep the dance, the Psy * trance of No conditioning.*
Seems a Paradox for a Yogi to go on WIFI. Why not?

*

She landed in a Sputnik from the old Soviet Union.
So lovely, irresistible with her jasmine & frangipani,
garlands of flowers entwined in Soyuz's golden hair.
"Don't think you have to do anything to make me happy"
Positive Independence ~ "Walkin' your talk is everything"
"I don't have much resistance either!" Wonderful ~
I gave up, we made love by the seaside every day

Future Shows

She's really fashion Conscious!
Tribal, exotic hippie, surrounded by physical beauty.
Golden skin in a string thong ~ You offer your body.
"Now I know what a Rainbow is!"
"How to live together"
They heard an OM going around the Planet
Tuning in with the festivals, living in Nature.
Our experience with Suns ~ everyday seeds,
frequency of a sacred geometry, yantra tattoo.
Good for your body, harmony in a Heart.
What do you like to make?

*

Unconscious, medieval Timbuktu from which Century?
'Rainbow Hotel' & 'Paradise Ayurvedic Pharmacy'
Many, many little steps ~ to Consciousness!
"Hey, I'm awaiting a baby from you"
"What is your name?" Super Ego.
A 'Hitler Lock' App. downloaded on the Computer.
Friendship ~ no more separation, open Internet.
Don't eat me, eat yourself.
Transformation ~ of the water
Crystals giving the information.
Silver for protection, gold to Shine out.
We're all waiting for the next level ~
'but my electrode's a little thinner than his!'
Allowance Process, brings you back to nature.
To allow yourself to be in the current.
No Judgments, straight in ~ flowing.
How you react on a Roller coaster…
Screaming ~ surrender to its laughter.
Open up your heart, so strong, direct.
Mystical floating ~ Spiritual Dimension.
Hungry for Life > Inshallah < What's it mean?

Throbbing Prop Up

Why pay ~ Any Attention ~ to it, maybe I shouldn't Mind?
Can't help seeing a beautiful pussy & not a Sex chakra!
'A Whale of a Time' ~ but not for this World's Baleines!
1000's of Fin, Minky & Humpbacks for Scientific Research!
1998, Low Copy No.- DNA evidence hadn't been Invented.
Now Ultra Sensitivity of technology, it's not an 'Absolute'!
No one's sanctioned for the Mistaken Murder of a Brazilian!
What's happening to the spinning Rhetoric? Ask the driver!

*

The TruTH

'The Bigger the lie the more people believe it.'
The Goddess had her 1st nervous breakdown.
My sister was a freedom fighter.
Wiser is less stress in this Goa Resort.
Full Power not the cods wallop ~
'The Universe will make it available to you'

*

Ask the Code

Wake Up, Wake Up, a Wake Up Call; For You!
"Settle down into that straight & narrow jacket.
'If there is a God what the Hell is S/he for?'
They see it but don't want to see through it.
Do one on the Pandemic destructive weapon!
"I don't want to become Anything ~
why is there any need to explain it?"
Letters, ripples in Pools of Water

*

It's just there because that's what came out the spout ~
If you don't want to Package & Commercialize Yourself
You can do what you like ~ be a stream of Consciousness
Don't need to answer anything, being Creative ~
don't let this Coercive State Censor you at all, ever!
Would that offend someone? You're Toast!

'You're a Whistler?' ~ 'No I Whistle'

Pretty Open Minded, took a room at the Shiva Motel.
Total wacko drama; New Modern Uber So. Cal.
She likes Jesus a lot ~
About that Big Pie in the Sky.
No piety, no humility; We're Right, You're Wrong!
"Give us a new business"
You're a Wind-up clock waiting for your Time to Ring.
'Give me the strength to accept things I cannot Change'
The all knowing is the all knowing ~ and is it Real?
All part of whose big Cosmic plan, your sins washed away.
"Never having to take responsibility for yourself." "Argh!"
People craving Perfection to attain the Perfect state ~
contrary to the infinite chaos, 'disorder' in the Universe ~
It gives them Control tools, their 1% belief, a little relief.
Reception, no reception in Laxmanjulla Rishikesh.
"that's a fuckin' cool spider"

*

Stereotype Eyes ~ Closed

All religious thoughts of Infinity since the 1st sunrise ~
Appeasing the supreme power, sacrificing the kids dear!
'The Big Yahweh in the sky' "Yeah fuck off with all violence"
Only seeing 'My Way' as the Right way; 'The Chosen Ones!'
Validity; ripping through their 'inferiors' in dead, refugee slums.
Preaching to the poor, uneducated, pushing through a jihadi
eye of the needle ~ in the narrowest streets of old Jerusalem.
No room in the Mosque for the Infidels; Absolutely No room
in Heaven for you not living up to The /My Holy expectations.
What the f… is a 'gentile' ad infinitum, nothing ~ Is True.
Whatever they say I'm not one of those 'Chosen' by You.
Still Torturers in this World of 'Extraordinary Renditioning'
Supported by Hypocritical 'UN. Democratic' Governments.
Because their Spin doctors call me 'sinner' doesn't mean
I AM

Last Tango

All these f... scenes, she shoots him ~
(A masterpiece)
that's my dream woman, what an end!

*

No Need to change

Anthropological tools were already there; a good Club!
People might start to Think; we're Perfect as ChAOS.
John's Gatling Gun, 50 Injuns just dropping like flies.
Don't touch my Shining armour....
We're the same everywhere; Complete lies, this the Myth
exporting to Global masses, people eating up that Shit!
The Chronicler, didn't want to be ~ A Noble Laureate.
Keeping the Ultimate Power 'Apocrypha'

*

'The Godfather!'

Urban Radical, there's no truth
to any of It, it's all Myth of US.
Ethymology no enthymology

*

'Ahimsa'

An Imploded Love Star
turning into a black hole.
How much Integrity do we have?
Civil Collective Schizophrenia
Sartre told them to f... off didn't want to be
that sort; can't have 'no' Violence!
Capital White & black trash
Cookin' Speed in bath tubs
all the nurses against him.
Taking out Ads; a Perfect Mistake....
the way it's supposed to be ~ 'be as it is'
The Big Real Mistake.
Hitler Goose-stepping into Mother Russia!

<u>No Accountability just the illusion of dots</u>

Being not doing ~ blip blip blip….

"I never realised how powerful it was
to let go"

Let Love Come

'Understanding You Are Your Own Creator'

Manifesting a beautiful garden with Eve

*In tune * in time*

10101010101010010101001010101010011010101010101
10101010101010010101001010101010011010101010102

Heaven ~ Idea of the future, crystal children…

"It's all about Oneness" ~ "Is this Paradise?"

Waiting for the time, for the wave now

The Vision is there

Vibrating through us

10101010101010010101001010101001101010101010101
10101010101010010101021010101001101010101010101
10101101001010010101010010101010011010101010101

"There is no evidence to suggest from the 25 Million lost
records that Your Information, has fallen into criminal hands"

Authority speaking but we're losing trust in your Incompetence!

*

Gestapo's $2 billion on Research.

The Ships, the Ships are coming!

I don't particularly like the word 'Sacrificial'

"My God is ready for his Meat!"

"The light had changed for her too"

Poor man deluded with Untested Winged Migration.

"Repenting from the Heart" ~ dropping a nightmare!

A little boy on Hiroshima & a fat man on Nagasaki

*

Philosophy

not much good at thinking

The Reality Check

Unfolding Petals!

Setting it up so he doesn't expect any bad vibes in his life ~
Planting seeds of good Karma, morality; in his meditation.
Not provoking demons, terrifying your imagination, scared
of your own shadow and fearful of anyone else's 'unusual'
behaviour because you've given your Mind this Power over
*your sense of who you are, lost the Independence of Your*self.*
Like seeing nature full of dangers, animals, plants insects, reptiles,
& inhuman, uncivilised cannibals, flyin' phobias in A I. Spacesuits.
Radium fish, tsunamis, earthquakes, swamps, bacteria, viruses
Savage sounds in the night, things you can't see.
Now you've Identified it ~ 'separate to the whole'
it exists, it has a life of its own, an Identity conditioning you!
I want this, I don't want that, I love you, I hate you, I Am/Not.
Mind playing tricks all the time, being attached, detached, smashed.
Your God, my God, no God, Yin & Yang, fully dual relativity!
Don't want to get outta bed or even go to bed, switching on
the News, hear about another Terrorist blowing up a plane
with exploding shoes, seems life is all about Win & losing!!!
Why be so frightened of Solitary Confinement? Living by the sword!
Mind games taking over the subject of who we truly are in Space!
Fears of disorders, fears of feelings, you've created your Minds,
created Karma. OK the hunter needs to 'Know' what he's up
against to survive, rather than children who've grown up
'Instinctively or as a poet Intuitively' in the natural bush.
All this psychological 'real' advice or doctrines of Infinity.
Seven types of this brain, 52 characteristics of that Mind,
then there's Quantum, entangled, particle, mega personalities!
Telling you to Beware of this type of action, thinking about this,
feeling that, plus she took it All and went to Live Abroad with our
daughter. On the NEWS, 'The Allies just blew up a Wedding party
with Cluster bombs, carpeting Afghanistan in bloody uranium daisies.
Being the 'Noble Savage' from the Garden of Eden,
but my Wife just fucked someone else

<u>Not Correct</u>

"It's life after death ~ does the Mind Yield?"
Ripe bananas, don't forget we're Stardust...
Forget about history; mirroring myself that's all.
It's all Vibrational healing ~
Invoke the frequency to come in
Alchemic process in the Unmanifest
You don't have to live it out ~
Your Mind will give ~ it to you?

*

Typical of the Madness
'Farcical Freedom Fries'
Ignorant, condescending with their foot in their oversized mouth.
Only 4% of their people travel, out of a box; like it Best here!
Tired of the bullshit, keeping the TV. on all day in cynical UK.
Nothing else to do, lost the will to live ~
$500 billion in debt; What's the Interest on that one darling?
Canada & Australia never signed the Kyoto Agreement either!

*

Coming back to Centre ~ balancing in tune
Coming from the deepest part of the Ocean.
A valley full of Candles alight at night
Fairy enchanted space with sexy angels
Stop lookin' for it ~ it'll find you.
Sowing your own seeds
"Put my foot right in it"
Until you know it ... Who is this Authority and Why?
Unconsciousness magnified by Crusaders with swords,
Killing each other in the market square for religious relics!
Should we be recognising each other as Gods?
Because there's only One infinity shining inside us ~
Unconditional Love (in the 4th Dimension of your heart)
Wisdom flowing ~You are a little Planet in Space

Heart beatings in the Jungle

Limbo dancing in a labyrinth of false teeth.
She was Mad but liked to fuck me silly!
Swallowed all the evidence, Jafna Cakes,
but those pills were for suicidal Tamil Tigers,
harder to chew than a Sri Lankan Ouroboros.
Met those Cloned glow in the dark cats in the pet shop.
Pagans coming in by the boatload

*

Mark of Cog 366

Two snails copulating &
Insect emotion is a Real thing.
Bob Marley's posthumous Nobel Prize.
Time to check out ~ Multiple entry Visa
Not for the diabolical creators of an axis of evil!
I don't want them coming for you in the night.
Not going to tattoo my rebellious hand until retired.
Never answer that; What do you write?
What does it mean; figure it out yourself
& don't stare at me.
"I'd never do that!"
"& I'd never wear that much makeup"
"What business is it of yours?"

*

OBEYING

Cog - obeys - cog
cog - fears - cog
cog - worships - cog
cog - consumes - cog
cog - submits - cog
Mantras at the back of my head ~
That's how I see it, always like that!
Have that little coq on freewheelin'

*Black * White*

Creation of disorder ~ All about the Cosmic Balance.
No such thing as 'detached', detached from what?
'To be or not to be' ~ It's a Full Power Celebration!
As soon as they Shut off Your Mind & Your Conscious
that's when they put their ideas in, more conditioning.
Let go of the extremes ~ embraced by a whole heart.
*Sitting there in infinite * eternal unboundless Space*
Listening to someone tell you what to do ~ all day!
'Have a taste of your own bullet it's coming back to you'
"Looking for Codeine 4, not cow dung"

*

Dissolves No Lines

"Nice watching the Predators" ~ he said.
Plenty of female Predators to fight back.
Why fuck up very good travelling sex ~
with a relationship? just another 'Control tool'
The Red Bandits' bad luck just a drop in the Ocean....
Letting material instinct override a 30 million year humming bird.
Heat Up your own Vibration ~ on the Inside
I Love that Stuff

*

Why do Wildebeest & migrating Zebras still cross rivers
full of Crocodiles? Separating from it, the Mind's Forms.
Resonating ~ going off, picking out the objects of illusion,
trying to shut the Mind off, realizing its hypnotic egoism!
Keep it going, don't need to detach ~ ***just to be*** ** Realism.*
Living ~ thoughts at the top of your head, making the whole.
Nothing to fear of your physical death only a process of dying.
Essential particle energy reflecting ~ its very high frequencies.
Just be with essence ~ existence, I was when I was conceived.
Can't put words to vibrations ~ Nature's omnipresent program.
"I don't exist, we're the drop in the Ocean
the drop is the Ocean!"

*Spiral*ling Optimist*

Facial reconstruction ~ Eye Expert
Biometric Conductivity of the Energy
Who knows what Truth is ~ working with shadows?
Just a word we Created (like everything else).
Integration ~ has to come
tried to understand all those Masquerades.
'Bye bye Whale, bye, bye Yangtze dolphin.'
Without Intrinsic Trust there is really nothing.
That phone call that never, never came, never.
"They'd make that sacrifice for us because I'd do it for them"
What does all that Love mean without the respect and trust?
Intuitively ~ that says I should have listened to my Instinct,
*to the feelings in the guts, in the heart * of my Merkaba!*

*

Surreal it's the real deal

I'd fallen in to Love with Gold for a Heart ~
One of those epics, yes, it's always changing.
She dumped him; did you know how cruel that was?
Learning the teaching that it's all relativity, always changes.
Tries to give more positive feelings, being happy not greedy.
"The more you give the more they take." Is there honesty?
'The Postman Always Rings Twice'; where's Juliet, Romeo?
'Spellbound' 'In Shock Corridor' 'In the House of Spirits'
How did those two smart crabs get up the stairs and into
your subconscious? Who's one step above the Flintstones?
You'll need a China visa before you can visit forbidden Tibet!
People are naturally competitive, that's a model they give us.
"If they hate me, they'll fear me!"
The masses seem to want another Cult of Personality,
they'll never treat each other equally, Monsignor Berlusconi.
They like to be Ruled over!
The Queen's Speech is on before Finding Nemo & Shrek 2!
Living the movie, this movie keeps getting better and better

Raw Unveiled Courage

Playing Percy Sledge & Al Green in Appalachian Prisons!
People will finally wake up in the USA; hung up by greed.
Time for Breakfast, lot of people felt conned; Your God ~
Zappa came from the 60's, wheat grass & aloe communes.
Lobster renaissance ~ Ontological Existentialism, LSD Free.
Divided in Society; sitting, standing on the crown of your head.
*Product of our environment, MDMA * DNA. many triggers.*
The Romantic fallacy that we're born good
Twiddling with a Lucid Bad Brain

*

Nix with a Vengeance

While Nixon was carpeting Laos & Cambodia with Bombs.
He was also after ('wow, I Love everybody!') Dr. Leary!
*Prescribing Psychic*delices to, 'turn on tune in drop out'*
Illuminating himself, Illuminating a lot of other people too.
You can't have eliminated populations; lights of reason?
Acid is where you're at, taken it in Eden with lovely Eva.
*Wanting to Love everyone in the Universe * of course ~*
Such a strange World, can you Imagine such a powerful
tool being used to Control your heart, mind, free spirit?
Such a powerful experience, so believable taking over ~
from Religions, Politics, Ego, who orders whom - Reality?
Get a number and get in line! The shit people believe,
can you Imagine dosing them with Acid?
Helping others turn on, living by my truth. Knowing Life,
dealing with your broken toe but with less depression.
Comfort for the masses Mother, leading us into the valley.
Earth taking revenge on this bad energy beach.
Take the most fantastic Illusion you can Imagine
"We successfully cloned everybody earlier today"
A monkey with a number, a battery in the Jungle.
If your wife falls down would they pick her up again?
One of the reasons we left that country on a jet plane

Clear burning oil from Hemp

"No money in the cure, only in Prevention ~ of disease, death!
"I've invented the automobile, you can invent the gas to drive it"
"I don't follow orders anymore"
"If I buy this Fungi Magico factory in Kodaikanal,
why do I want to do anything else?"
Got to be True to yourself here...
"You're free, you've got to make a decision"
Trapped inside a wheel of Paradise

*

A New Beginning

Tracing the memory of a Revolution ~
Keep moving keep breathing keeping being.
Unravelling the Magnolia blossom in the air ~
telepathy into a billion particles of Qasar string,
let the jungle in, let the monkeys in with red hair.
Being controlled by a smart alpha dog ~ only a dog!
I had no idea she was Top dog & you were the Slave.
The one who filled the bowl, the one who licked her plate.
She wanted grass & running free
My bedroom's not your domain, my pussy feels.
She rules the house; "dude this is My Spot!"

*

'Squeeze & Crush'

.... found a baby tortoise crossing the street.
A jealous pet Python crushes her on the honeymoon.
How old is the programming of that animal?
"I wouldn't want to be in a spaceship with her"
Look at those little furry horns!
Always the same, must be other ways to move this energy.
'The News' Car bombings, 50 dead every day in Baghdad!
Nature doesn't need miracles, humans do but it's up to you.
The Universe has to have space for mutation, evolution ~
just how the force works ~ reading exploding Sunspots

Karma Lust Lesson

You desire ~ You deserve this fuckin' shit.
So enjoy your free choice of experiencing…
Allowance ~ of 100 million years of Vertebrates,
with dung beetles, flowering plants, now genetically
engineered mosquitoes put into the toxic mix; out there.
You have no more importance than that chunk of rock!
"As soon as you think that you can explain it, you can't"

*

'Ow Now'

Bloody dangerous socket on the descending, blazing rocket!
Pay attention, rioting brown cows on little Vagator beach.
The World is his doughnut, he can do whatever he likes
for the rest of his life, fact from fiction, from intuition ~
from superstition, discovery of Pegasus' flights of fancy.
An invitation to a Priestess with her own devoted Love cult.
'The most perfect lie is the one closest to the Truth'
"Hi Kids it's ~ Crack Time!"

*

Tiger Shanti Bohemians

"If it's Not harming anyone do what you like and enjoy
the freedom." ~ I get a lot of Peace and Quiet here…
Good karma exists as a concept, don't make it a golden cage.
Mind does Not exist in Reality, creating Illusory Objects.
Forms, Live and let Live ~ isn't that your password or Mantra?
Putting it into Neural-neutral, what are we supposed to do?
Reflect the best for all, don't try to pre-judge ~ stay in the now.
We need to be detached, ask at the Kaleidoscopic Temple.
Who 'Masterminded' the Massacre at Srebinica?
'There is nothing new under the Sun'
'You are everything to my Ego darling'
Is this Paradise?

*Magus * Inspiration*

If you think you're meditating, you're not,
that's where eternity is ~ it's already here.
Don't need to die for it!
Not even thinking about it ~ put it off, now.
You just fuckin' know, witness Mind's game.
Be humble enough to admit you don't know.
More & more control as you peel the Union.
People once so much outside themselves.
That Meditation Inside Zone, lost for words.
The White Cone,
if you don't find yourself there you're there.
Brain's running like a strobe ~ viewing your
disappearance, synapse firing a different way.
"YES I NEED TO TAKE A PAINKILLER"
You don't have to sell the Truth
You don't have to tell the lies.
Goodbye Red Couch

*

Morphine Patch Placebo

As long as you don't suffer from your beliefs ~
Confusing Channeling, Mary Magdalene in Atlantis.
Prattling on psychosis, he's got the facts and figures....
Traditional & mythology, coming up with your own belief system,
having neither fact nor theory, but accepts VISA & NSA Prism!
You'll get the bill later, with a massive interest charge,
every moment overdue, ran over a busload of nuns!
Outside their remit, advanced Yogi, the whole of Zen
binding atoms about being, not rushing around about.
All wacked on awakening their Kundalini; stop threats to the Soil!
Every housewife in Duluth waiting on the harmonic ~ convergence

*

Idea
not to have any

*Poly * morphs*

So many more Predators, they put their flesh on display.
I've never seen apathy like this in my life! Fully controlled….
Wide eyed disciples, sexual enlightening then you're fuckin me,
doesn't all end with him, you're the divine ego, what yu gonna do?
I like the whirring dervishesssssssss ~ inviting them for mint tea.

*

Anticipation Just Began

"There's no such thing as bad karma,
there's no such thing as good karma"
Pipe dreaming accepted by the masses ~
It just is; Inevitability doesn't need any belief &
who's cruising around the blue Sun of Galaxy #99?
Would you like to propagate some species dude?
"No, no I want a stray free spirit!"

*

Dropouts, Oh never Mind!

Learning how the inner World works
Integrated a renaissance education,
experiences of the It, super Id, Jesus.
If you can't assimilate ~ that's it Man!
Take off your clothes and get Paid…
Latvian lap dancing in Cardiff every afternoon.
Nothing wrong with that, we're in a Celtic land
blonde 5 foot 2" & all bubbly

*

How to survive an Oppressive, high energy workload!
Buzzing up, there's a Wasps nest; bad to be in prison.
Nice to be on other end of the Spectrum; I actually cared.
Working for a reason, not loving it is a complete schism.
Boundaries of giving & receiving, my shit, did it my way
without anyone questioning me; finding Independence.
Living in some flow now ~
The Theatre of Life is thriving

<u>Placating them</u>

Fine Line between the customer and showing respect.
Telling someone to 'fuck off' while smiling (at them).
Adrenalin in full flight, at least I'm by the seaside ~
A view of the city skyline, beach, open horizon, stars.
Looking out the other direction ~ it's a new perception.

*

Perfect

Opening the door
of the Universe
found that Space
without trying
Organic ally

*

<u>Mindfulness</u>

Based on clear and open ~ free flowing Meditation
generating vibrations taking you to Mindlessness ~
Subconsciously we can leave
don't have to let go or anything
just be Open to its beingness.
** UNCONDITIONAL LOVE **
Resonating with higher frequencies

*

<u>LSD. 25</u>

You've got a lot of filters to bypass
*Mindfulness * Mindlessness, bottom line is just words....*
Alchemical delusion, I don't know, just trying to observe it,
if there is something ~ 'Collective' out there in the fusion.
If they buy into that they're building their own Control tools.
Let's go back to Napa Valley and have a glass of Pinot noir.
What's happening for you at the moment ~ feel the sensations.
Redefining 'Real'- "nothing is Real." The dying words of a Sufi ~
"Nothing is Real, everything is permitted"

People don't work like this.

Repressed energy, locked up in a country of undesirables.
Drug testing while you're driving, took the responsibility
for being stoned! Taking the risk, doing it Underground,
blasting through your neighbourhood; check that out!
"If there's a God what the Hell is s/he for?" As I lay dying.
Relaxing in a strange room, emptying yourself for sleep ~
Sin is just a matter of words to them, salvation is words too,
delivering strong beans across country, needed new laws.
Perfect Room for mistake, not promised any eternal Nirvana.
There has to be chaos, randomness, a room for 'disorder'
Making Perfect Sense

*

No Hokey Pokey

Being Conscious being Present being Intuition.
How High do I have to elevate my foot? Feel it ~
vibing with nothing? You're more energy than that.
Is my Mind directing what's coming from Spiritual?
Essence filling it with acceptance, then you know.
"He wants others to share in his pain, it's a Habit"

*

Great Respect

Don't piss around and he shot himself!
Made sense to him.
Mind really has to be unbalanced for that!
Clean up your own shit, blinkers keep it Toxic.
Nice chips in the chai shop but Baba please change
to Organic packaging!

*

Free Razor

Loyalty to Gillette; with free Coke sun umbrellas.
Behind a Special Counter ~ In a special fridge.
Even taking a loss to get any customer!
'The profit's on the Cola not the Burger'

Inspired by True Events

Detaché, attaché, why not have them both, les deux?
So Very difficult to live by these High moral principles!
What do I know? Moment to moment, beyond words.
Live by your heart, don't fuck with the monkey mind.
The Devil's two best friends are alcohol & coke; OK
let's include Bad weapons & greed & exploitation
& Crack houses in inner city ghettoes bro! Word!
Monkeys grabbed my nuts at the Hanuman Temple.
Why not? Absolutely, why not?

*

The Government is closing us down.
Such a loss, such a pain, my beauty.
Irish ~ "They dig a mean tunnel"
"Most of what matters in our lives
takes place in our absence ~"
They're focusing on the bullshit not on the Brilliance!
How do you really know, getting rid of the mad Taliban,
evangelism purposely destabilising the shell shocked!
"You'll be picking up your teeth with broken fingers dude"
Lucky you survived that bad boy Hitler's blitz, a lot didn't!
Chemical warfare but not from Venus' spinning flytraps ~
plants communicating through pheremones' lovely perfume,
infatuated, mesmerized, unbelievable, her first attraction.
Killed by an anonymous flying drone!

*

Captain Crunch, Never ever forever ~
Moses has a big fiery bush talkin' back to him!
King Ganesha carving the Ganges with his tooth
And Jesus built my hot rod! Unselfconsciously ~
Chimping out, the Rage against the Machines!
On your deathbed, listening to the jungle at night.
*Perfect Psyche*sociology, tripping silver masks.*
Killing in the nude

Living Meditation Oneness

All Mind Games
Come to Goa to defrag, to default, delete.
Mind already fucked enough
"Hi Pam, no abusive sex ~ and your five sisters!"
What's a Spanish Romantic Amora?
Hot blooded hood!

*

'In Love Baba!'

Better than Ron Jeremy any day of the week
better than Peter North by a long hard chalk.
Top Shelf ~ Baba G. Spot from the black country!
"Don't walk on the beach at night alone ~
the prostitutes will be all over you in Bahia"

*

Pot Holes Myth

I can't drive my scooter fast especially across the flooded padi fields.
Retarded Cliché: The World's Largest Democracy, Indian feudalism!
Temple of my soul, turning into Sacred Geometry beyond dualisms.
Now I'm lookin' at the sunset a different way, the full Moon,
the Stars, tropical fish on a reef, shy insects in love,
the Martian crystal fairy from upper Kazakhstan ~
Energetic Universe

*

Sharing

Don't hide your treasures, jewels deep in your Yoni.
Families of 50 monkeys sitting watching the Sunset.
A Big Transmutation, making the Pyre by herself.
Walking through the snow over the Himalayas
with her Lover's ashes in a Milk churn

*

The drug

Snowing poppy seeds on our streets ~
And Coke is the Real thing to Charley!

Internal Ginseng Memo

Stop missing the present ~ Revolutions.
'Clockwork Oranges' in your corner shop.
Little Alex beating the crap out of little Ali
Somethings take time, who has the answer to it?
Slow season, unlucky man playing Chechen Roulette!
It's a fun game with glamorous Eve from St Petersburg.
*Psy*chic surfing ~ psy*chics fucking off to Chapora ~*
China's a part of Walmart, a warehouse in Shanghai,
just like the old days but with different opium dealers.
Shooting baby ants, wiping out a brand new generation!
Computers Ruling their Life, don't lose it ~ natural reality.
A I. Pentiums, video games, X boxes, making connections.
Smelling pink, wild Roses on a walk along a country lane ~

*

*108 Rounds * of Reality TV*

'I don't need those dreams'
What's it say?
"Go to Sleep"
A mantra…

*

Ecuador

I achieved one ambition…
"Stayed here for the mango season"
'My dream, My dream, My dreams'
………………………………
………………………………
………………………………
………………………………
'Maria full of Grace'
'Smell Proof Turkey Bags'
And a Merry Christmas to You. B. Ocean ~
"Get out of my dreams and into my car"
World Peace over easy scrambled

Lock-In Somewhere

"If I was doing telepathy I'd be guiding them
onto my crotch (I mean face, he said)……
Two tits, a hole and hopefully a Heartbeat, easily Pleased;
Is it Miller Time?" "Sure Is Chillum time!"
Brunettes from the South, Blondes from the North,
just accepting it's happening. Step out of the body,
dissolving the Mind ~ not negating it, just
Surrendering to Synergetic Serendipity

*

*Healthy * Wealthy*
Got Time
to Spend

*

*Sun Lover * Amoré de Sol*

*Like Minded * People Living freely*
*A tribal sense * coming together ~*
at Sunset on the beach with fire dancers ~
At Sunrise with the fishermen returning home.
No more need of Formal vibes ~ set in reinforced concrete.
Enjoy nature's vibrant colours of verdant, monsoon padi fields.
Enjoying parties of ecstasy, enjoying flowing together, you & me.
Enjoying fully being here now

*

Horsemen of the Apocalypse

Don't want to work in a factory if I can help it….
'His ex-girlfriend had her hood pierced with a spiral bangle.'
*Getting it anywhere * everywhere Imaginable and even more!*
Let's hope they're the true Freedom fighters, Mr. Contra President.
Nothing's greater than a bunch of people living, ruling themselves…
We didn't ask you for a Railway, to teach us English, or bleed us dry!
Didn't ask you to turn up to 'Divide & Conquer' us either, who would?
Unless you're from some distant territories with no human feelings left,
no women, no horses, mirrors, dynamite; gravity, empty creed of greed

'The Olde Pub'.

'The Saintly Church of England'
Spreading the seeds, oh my God!
On dodgy withering, deformed, rickety legs…
Their Protection, their Revelation, Justification, absolution!
In a Mad System of 'Reality Shows' The World's Weather,
Hollyoaks, Sport, The News, 24/7, Big Brother, X Factor!
A WARning Shot ~ Across your brow! Pay Attention mate!
Top Up your Private Pension, ISA, Medical, life Insurance.
"just in case it could be You" but it's 14 Million to 1 against!
Laws for everything, they make them Up as they go along;
they're not in favour of being free, having Fun Intentionally!
Manifesting it all on a Platinum Credit Card, Bling, bling.
"Happiness of Goa is my tribal church ~"
Casted, no choice in a Dictatorship!
'In Spiritual there is No Caste'
Choices of my Mind; how Dictated to are You?
Proving It, an Alarm/bell Tolling; "Can't Not do it!"
If you're Exploited and Accept it, having no choices;
don't know if that's good, ask a sex trafficed soul.
'A Pay-off at the End!' Plug in another Program.
Can't Distinguish between Right & Wrong
of food, of dualities, Separation & Unity,
Dividing & Ruling & harmony for those…
dealing with five generations of traumatizing Horror …
turning up on Your Street with an empty cardboard box!
Mitigating circumstances of course, ask the super-d'elite.
Give them all a Job, give them Meditation, whatever is ~
Sewed his arms & legs back on at the Children's Hospital.

*

Forensic Nightmare

When you wake Up ~
in the Middle of the night
And the Pope's Not there!

Rubbish Destiny

They really need a fuckin' Thunderbolt from Vishnu
when you see our Nandi eating another plastic bag!
Dumped it on the beach, over any wall, not yours -
Philosophy; 'giving it back to Ma Earth' Danyavad!
Moron, cretin, washed up syringes in your garden!
Disgusting, living in a tip, "come on Durga wake up"
Let's clean up this shit hole given to you as pristine.
It's a grotesque slum, end of any 'Civilised' World.
Landing at Mumbai somehow people still can smile.

*

Indian flexi ~ time

Reading Braille by the touch of your labial lips.
Rather have seen golden beaming spaceships
hovering on the horizon ~ not Christian crosses
on fortified Galleon sails, anchored inside the reef.
When our tribe walked out of the forest in chains ~

*

Lovely Chaos

Look at that Pure blue sky ~ I wonder
Or? 'Taking the Straight and Narrow'
"They don't care, if the cash is there!"
fiery little girls
My sweet Eva

*

Weaving, watching a mugging in Calangute

We've come to Expect clean water running from our tap.
Electricity, energy to provide everything. Fresh food
in the shop, safety with your neighbours. I wonder ~
if there's such a thing as a 'One way street' in India?
The Matrix, holding this Mind, body & soul together ~
Opening to Synchronicity is a fresh morning breeze

'An Executive Decision'

Whose giving everyone in the World clean drinking water?
Rulers' Eugenics, Dianetics, Deception, Black Psych-Ops!
They say Hitler was one of Aldous Huxley's biggest fans!
Too many children die! Did you see 'Zeitgeist' 'Thrive' 'Illuminati'?
He gave that bird a bit of righteous sperm. Implanted, embedded.
FEMA. Camps, Moslem gulags on the horizon, coming soon.
20% of US. on Anti depressants ~ "Who's giving them Drugs!"
Who is making such a shitty environment & Praying to Satan?
New World Order's giving people aspirations, nightmares, fear.
To be ~ Indebted; brainwash the masses, with no free time ~
Forced Labour, US Prison Rights, 25 years for Pirating a dvd!
George W. Bush's dictatorship totally smashed the Constitution;
Patriot Acts, Under the Care of the USA Empire, Government!
System designed to work or to enslave? Ask the Bildebergers!
'Les droits humains' ~ gone up in smoke, see Prisonplanet.com

Pharma Corporations' 'Codex Alimentarius' ~ Seed weaponary!
USA. $20 Trillions in Debt, can you repeat please? To whom?
What's the Interest on that dear? Get the calculator son.
Get Real the Ice is Melting at the steaming Polar caps!
The Bank of England & Federal Reserve are Privately owned,
by Whom? Welcome Emperors Rothschild, Rockefeller et al.
Which Cartel Controls the Monetary Fund, the World Bank, BIS?
Setting their/our Interest Rates; Indebted, in servitude to WHOM?

*

*"Love * gives you Energy ~ It moves"*

He got away in a Psychedelic Rainbow car ~
be yourself, be who you are, be who you want.
Death ~ 'believe in the Miracle frequencies'
"The end is coming ~ from Sense Perception"
*It's nobody's fault * LIVING IS MEDITATION.*
Life is being Alive ~ belonging to the Universe
It's All One nature ~ go wherever you want to go

ABOUT SUNNY JETSUN

*Inspired by the sixties Sunny started traveling the world in 1970. His spiritual journey on the hippie trail to India took him through ~ San Francisco, Los Angeles, London, Amsterdam, Paris, Vancouver, Sidney and Kathmandu to Varanasi. His arrival on the sub-continent ~ was the beginning of writing autobiographical verses capturing his travel experiences, encounters with remarkable people and his quest for self-realization. Combining experimentation with drugs, sex, rock & roll, art, meditation, Love and life in general. Sunny started to open up to a multi-dimensional Universe. He lived the mantra, "Turn on, tune in, drop out" realising Mind's-illusions, inspired by deeper feelings of holistic nature, empathy * energy & Space.*

Over four decades Sunny has written and published 28 books of poetry, created over one hundred paintings, traveled the World and considers his masterpiece to be his daughter. He has spent the past fifteen years in Goa ~ India inspired by the freedom to experience and idealism of human consciousness.

Sunny Jetsun books and art are available on the web at:

Website: www.sunnyjetsun.com
Facebook: www.facebook.com/sunnyjetsun
Amazon: www.amazon.com/author/sunnyjetsun
Smashwords: www.smashwords.com/profile/view/sunnyjetsun

www.ingramcontent.com/pod-product-compliance
Lightning Source LLC
Chambersburg PA
CBHW020509030426
42337CB00011B/296
9781910363430